A Pinch of This

est moi,
cuit

A Pinch of This

And a Soupçon of That

Marie Pietri Kilpatrick

Foreword by
James J. Kilpatrick

Oxmoor House®

Book Division of Southern Progress Corporation
P.O. Box 2463, Birmingham, Alabama 35201

Library of Congress Catalog Number: 87-060992
ISBN: 0-8487-0824-5
Manufactured in the United States of America
First Printing 1987

Executive Editor: Ann H. Harvey
Senior Foods Editor: Katherine M. Eakin
Production Manager: Jerry Higdon
Associate Production Manager: Rick Litton
Art Director: Bob Nance

A Pinch of This And a Soupçon of That

Editor: Olivia K. Wells
Editorial Assistant: Mary Ann Laurens
Designer: Jane Bonds
Illustrator: Dana Moore

To Bernice Pietri Nestor

Contents

FOREWORD

Somewhere in the family archives is a photograph of two fried eggs, sunnyside up, accompanied by a piece of toast and a strip of bacon, all nicely arranged upon a breakfast plate. The plate is wedding-present new. I am looking at these divine objects with hungry expectation. It is late September of 1942, and this is the first meal put upon our table by my bride of seven days, the preceding six days having been spent on a honeymoon at the old Deltaville Beach Hotel. We have returned to Richmond to take up residence in a small apartment at 2621 Stuart Avenue in the city's West End. The apartment is sparsely but lovingly furnished with one small sofa, one matching chair, one piano, and some bookshelves. The sofa and chair are on the installment plan; the piano we inherited; the shelves we made ourselves. The apartment has a galley kind of kitchen and a breakfast nook for four. It is here, cookingwise, that my life began.

I did not realize back in 1942 what glorious luck I had fallen into. My own mother, bless her, was a lovely and gracious lady, but during my boyhood she left all the cooking to Lizzie Shaw. Lizzie made epicurean corncakes for breakfast, but her culinary skills stopped there. This was Oklahoma cuisine. Subsequently I was exposed to fraternity house and boardinghouse menus at the University of Missouri. I entered upon matrimony knowing as little about good cooking as I know about overhead cams.

Throughout our courtship Marie had said almost nothing of the cooking art. The topic had barely arisen. Now it was time to face life. She began by facing the stove. As it transpired, she had learned a great deal about cooking from her grandmother and from her father. As a teenager she had mastered the apple pie. She had learned the magical tricks that go into a sausage sauce for spaghetti. She had learned to stuff and truss a chicken and to take whatever it is you take out of a leg of lamb.

More than this, she had developed a set of principles for cooking that she has followed ever since: (1) meals should be nutritious; (2) meals should be simple; (3) meals should be economical; and (4) meals should be pretty.

Each of the principles has a kind of subset: Let us not be fanatic about it, but let us give due regard to calories, cholesterol, vitamins, minerals, starches, and other such rules of dietetics. It is better to bake, broil, or sauté than to fry. Without the most compelling reason, such as doughnuts, never deep-fry anything. Without an indispensable need, never use sugar at all. Let us plan menus with an eye not only on tonight but also on the rest of the week. Leftovers need not look like leftovers. The right herbs and spices can transform a proletarian dish into a noble creation. Some dishes are better the next day. Male appetites are not exactly inexhaustible, but they are almost inexhaustible; therefore, let us put filling meals before the men of a family. Finally, let us equip our kitchen with the best knives we can afford, and let us keep them razor sharp.

I have enjoyed a husband's role in all this. I am the consuming, applauding audience. I am the cleaner-upper. Beyond that I function as a consultant. She asks, "Wouldn't you like baby lima beans with the trout?" I say, "Yes." I am Official Taster: "Is there enough cumin in the chili?" I am What's-a-Husband For: "Can you get the top off this jar of capers?" I am encouraged to baste or to stir, but never to put in seasoning myself. After my disastrous mutilation of our first Thanksgiving turkey, I have been forbidden to carve anything more complicated than a tenderloin of beef. Here I am not to be trusted.

These have been rewarding years in the kitchen and at the table. We have seen changes. Together we have gone from the iceman to the icemaker. We have grown up with the blender, the chopper, the tomato machine. During our early years of marriage, a milkman from Richmond Dairy used to bring fresh milk at 5:00 A.M. It came in bottles with onion tops to collect the cream; you don't see those wonderful bottles any more. During the war years, when beef, pork, lamb, butter, and baby food were hard to come by,

Marie learned to do inventive things with tongue, liver, chicken, fish, and beef hearts.

Along the way she has experienced a few disasters. In the early 1950s, we thought we might afford to hire a cook. It was a lamentable thought. Our first and only cook somehow managed to put a whole jar of sage into a turkey dressing, thus making the bird inedible. The cook survived the wrath of Little Vesuvius on that occasion, but a few days later we invited a distinguished magazine editor to dinner. (It was the late David Lawrence of *U.S. News & World Report.*) He arrived in a chauffeur-driven limousine. Marie had planned to put on the dog. It strained our budget, but she bought a fine Virginia ham and supervised its beautiful decoration. She had a yam soufflé, and she had other creations. The dinner went well and the after-dinner conversation was lively. Meanwhile, back in the kitchen, the cook took a fancy to the chauffeur, and the chauffeur ate all the leftover ham. There went our prospective ham mousse, and the next day there went the cook.

Such disasters have been few. As Marie acknowledges in her book, she is not much on cakes (though she is better than she thinks she is). She has no interest in Chinese, Japanese, or Bulgarian cooking. She has a positive prejudice against brussels sprouts. The fifty cookbooks in her kitchen library are strong on American, French, and Italian cuisine, and she adds constantly to her recipe file by a page-by-page scanning of *Southern Living* and other magazines.

In sum, we eat *good*. With a pinch of this and a soupçon of that, she raises cooking from a craft to an art. In this book she invites you to try your hand at her hand. Bon appetit!

JAMES J. KILPATRICK
White Walnut Hill
Woodville, Virginia

January 1987

ETIZING
OP

ONE

Grandmother

Grandmother was born and reared in a villa on the slopes of Mount Vesuvius. "Where the volcanic soil was perfect for the grapes," she would say, but of course she would say this in Italian. Speaking in English to my sister and me, she would recall that when Vesuvius erupted, the smoke and ash spewed up and toward the sea and just missed her villa and the vineyards. Inhabitants from the village below would climb up to the villa to seek shelter when the mountain became angry.

She was a tiny woman, barely five feet tall, but she made up in dignity what she lacked in height. She married young and came to America around 1885 to rear a family. Eventually they settled in Richmond, Virginia. They didn't exactly prosper, and their house near Belvedere and Cary streets was much smaller than her villa in Italy. It didn't matter. She always was known as La Donna Rosa, and a true lady she was. She took great pains in instructing me in manners and dress. Petticoats and ribbons had to be just so, and hair and hands and fingernails had to be sparkling clean for her inspection. She was calm and gentle and soft spoken. (Some of her calmness rubbed off on me, but perhaps not enough; our three boys have called me "Little Vesuvius" since the first time I erupted at their disorderly rooms.)

I was born in the small tobacco town of Wilson, North Carolina, the summer before Harding was elected in November. Among my earliest memories—apart from the unforgettable aroma of flue-cured tobacco—are memories of the train ride to Richmond to visit Grandmother. Those visits were frequent, and often I was left with my grandparents for a week or more.

There was a small Italian bakery near Grandmother's house, and often I trotted happily with La Donna to buy long loaves of fresh Italian bread. It took a while to make even a simple purchase, because Grandmother and Signora Fazzi exchanged bits of neighborhood gossip and inquired about each other's families. I couldn't understand their Italian, but I could understand their hands. Without hands they would have been speechless. If I were patient and quiet through all this conversation, Signora Fazzi rewarded me with one of her freshly baked almond cookies. Any small child would have stayed quiet under the motivation of a freshly baked almond cookie.

Grandmother was a superb cook. Her creed in life was never to be wasteful in the kitchen. She made marvelous dishes from leftovers and wonderful soups from almost anything. She insisted on buying the freshest and best meats and vegetables. Her loose translation of an Italian adage was, "Never buy anything cheap. You can't afford it."

Sometimes Grandmother would take me on the streetcar to the old Sixth Street market. The ride down Broad Street was interesting, but the market was exciting. It yielded to progress in the 1970s, but in the 1920s the market was a colorful two-block center of lively commerce. The sidewalks were lined with produce vendors, and the long buildings were filled with butchers' stalls and poultry counters. It was noisy and usually crowded, and I clung tightly to La Donna's hand. She would pause periodically to let me peek at the live ducks and chickens, and sometimes we would find rabbits.

Grandmother's favorite butcher was a jolly, rotund man who stood ankle-deep in sawdust before an enormous chopping block. His knives and cleavers gleamed with constant sharpening, and he cut each piece of meat with care. Grandmother believed that small children should be fed especially nourishing foods, and she would buy sweetbreads and tiny loin lamb chops for me. She would have the butcher slice paper-thin veal scaloppine and cut a leg of lamb for Sunday dinner.

After our long visit with the butcher, we moved on to the vegetable stalls where the farmers were often raucous, hawking their fresh corn, lima beans, green beans, and tomatoes, fresh-picked that very morning. La Donna would choose the vegetables with discriminating care. The beans had to be young and tender (she would snap one to find out), and the corn had to be juicy and not overripe (she would push aside the shucks and test a kernel with her fingernail). Tomatoes were inspected one by one, until she settled upon those that were perfectly red and firm. I waited impatiently while she made her choices, because last of all would be the Italian importing shop. Just to walk through the door was an experience of pure delight. Dried herbs hung in bunches from the ceiling; jars of black olives stood on the counter; a large glass-fronted icebox held cheese redolent of goats' milk, and the shelves were crammed with tins of anchovies, virgin olive oil, tomato paste, and pastas of all shapes and sizes. Grandmother always bought a small amount of alphabet pasta or egg pastina to put in the chicken soup she made for my lunch. She bought bunches of oregano and basil and always a healthy piece of Romano cheese. Signor Russo would reach into the candy jar and give me two Jordan almonds, "Uno per ciasuno mano." One for each hand.

Sunday dinner at Grandmother's was a gala affair. The round oak table was fitted with extra leaves and covered with a white linen cloth—a cloth so white and beautifully ironed it looked new though it was many years old. Grandpapa presided at the head of the table. He was tall, thin, quiet, and intimidating. He was a shoemaker by trade. I remember that his mouth usually was tightly compressed, perhaps from a lifetime of having it filled with tacks. He used to look at my sister and me with the studied perplexity of a tourist examining foreign coins, but he was never unkind. Other members of my mother's family encircled the table, too. There was roly-poly Uncle Frank, the bachelor uncle, along with Uncle Tony, the debonair one, and Aunt Virginia, prim and critical. Mother was flanked by my sister and me, and she always was a bit nervous that we might say or do something to displease Grandpapa. So long as we kept our mouths mostly closed, he smiled benignly at us.

Dinner started with pasta. The huge platter was brought to the table, and the delectable aroma of tomato sauce and Romano cheese wafted through the dining room. Grandpapa's two carafes of wine—one white, one red—were placed before him. With great deliberation he would measure out a little wine diluted with water just for me. My older sister inherited that spaghetti platter; I inherited the carafes.

After the pasta disappeared, Grandmother brought in the roast. Usually it was accompanied by tiny potatoes, and always there were three vegetables. Later came the salad, and finally the fruit. I don't remember that Grandmother ever made desserts. She probably was protecting Uncle Frank.

Her pastas, in the Italian tradition, were varied and many. She made plain tomato sauce for spaghetti, sausage sauce for rigatoni, and braciole in tomato sauce with spaghettini. We feasted regularly on lasagna. A very special sauce came with vermicelli, traditionally on Christmas Eve. It was considered a meal for fasting; no meat was served at dinner, only a green salad. I suspect that originally it was a peasant dish, but now it has become quite fashionable in Rome as an after-theatre meal any time of year.

Vermicelli con Olio e Acciughe

Cook one pound vermicelli or very thin spaghetti in *unsalted* water. The sauce will be salty. Heat one-half cup olive oil in a skillet; sauté three cloves of garlic for a couple of minutes. Remove the garlic. Add one can anchovies, drained, and mix and simmer until the anchovies dissolve. You can help the process along by mashing the anchovies with a fork. Drain the vermicelli; dump it back in the hot kettle and pour the anchovy sauce over it. Fluff and mix gently. Serve in flattish soup bowls or pasta bowls. Sprinkle liberally with Parmesan cheese.

Grandmother was introduced to oysters when she arrived in Virginia, but she regarded the usual oyster stew or oysters on the half shell as wholly lacking in imagination. True to her creative instincts, she invented an oyster sauce for linguine, which she served as a first course before Thanksgiving dinner. The recipe never has been put in writing but has been passed down through four generations. Sorry, but exact measurements are impossible.

Oyster Sauce

Heat one or two tablespoons olive oil in a large skillet, and sauté one sliced clove of garlic until brown. Discard the garlic, and sauté one onion, chopped, and one-half green pepper, minced, in the same oil until they are transparent. Add a one-pound can of Italian tomatoes, chopping them if they are whole. Cook about ten minutes, and add two tablespoons of tomato paste mixed with one-half cup of warm water. Add a healthy pinch of basil and salt and pepper to taste. Simmer ten or fifteen minutes more, or until the sauce cooks down somewhat. Drain one pint of oysters, and add the juice to the tomato sauce, stirring well. Bring the sauce to a boil, and add the oysters. Simmer until the oysters are warmed through and only slightly curled at the edges. Ladle the sauce over one pound of linguine cooked *al dente*.

Grandmother cooked the pasta in a large kettle. She usually salted the water and added a small amount of olive oil to keep the pasta from sticking together. I stood beside her while the kettle was bubbling and watched while she placed the pasta in the boiling water. She measured out one fistful per person to be served, and stirred vigorously for a minute or two. Soon she tested for doneness by lifting out two strands of spaghetti, one for her and one for me. We each tasted by biting the strand. She would declare the exact moment the spaghetti was done. It wasn't to be hard in the middle and never mushy in the mouth. The spaghetti was drained immediately and covered with one of her sauces. By the time I was six years old I had learned the meaning of *al dente*.

As with all of her pasta dishes, Grandmother's lasagna was a labor of love and a work of art. It requires hours to cook the sauce and to assemble the dish. Hungry children can demolish it all in minutes. But when time permits, it is a dish well worth the effort.

La Donna's Lasagna

Sauce: Coat the bottom of a large skillet with olive oil, and cook one-half pound of lean ground beef until it is no longer pink. Add one medium onion, chopped; one stalk of celery, minced; and one carrot, grated. Cook and stir until the vegetables are soft. Add a crushed clove of garlic, if you like. Add two cups of plum tomatoes. Chop or mash the tomatoes. Add a good pinch of marjoram and one of basil. Salt to taste. Cook and stir the sauce for ten or fifteen minutes, and add half a small can of tomato paste. Stir until the paste has become liquid and is no longer lumpy. Add a cup of dry white wine, and simmer the sauce for thirty or forty minutes.

Cheeses: Beat one egg, and beat in one-half pound of ricotta cheese and one-half cup of grated Parmesan cheese; set mixture aside. Slice thinly one-half pound of mozzarella cheese; set aside.

Noodles: Cook eight or ten lasagna noodles *al dente* and drain them. To avoid having burned fingers, plunge the noodles into cold water. Lightly oil a lasagna baking pan, and spoon in enough sauce to cover the bottom. Place a layer of noodles over the sauce (use your fingers for this job because a fork or spoon will break up the noodles), then a layer of the ricotta cheese mixture and the slices of mozzarella. Cover the layer of cheeses with more sauce. Repeat the layering process until all the sauce, cheeses, and noodles are used. Sprinkle the top with a little more Parmesan cheese, and bake in a moderate oven for thirty minutes or until the lasagna is very hot and bubbly. This recipe serves ten ordinary guests or three teenaged boys.

Grandmother's roasts always were tender and succulent. She knew how to judge a piece of beef, veal, or pork just by looking closely at the patterns of fat. Her Sixth Street butcher knew better than to offer her a roast that might look gorgeous in the counter but would be a disappointment on the table. One of her tricks with a leg of lamb was to marinate it overnight in red wine vinegar laced with garlic and basil. The next day she continued:

Roast Leg of Lamb

Remove the fell, the thin papery skin, and most of the fat. If the butcher hasn't done it for you, remove the shin bone below the joint. Place a peeled clove of garlic and a pinch of basil in the flap of meat, and pin up the flap with a poultry pin or two. Rub the leg with salt and pepper and a sprinkling of basil. If you wish, make two or three slits in the meat, and insert two or three cloves of garlic. Grandmother cooked the roast in a medium-to-slow oven, and it was always tender and moist. She knew from experience when the roast was done. I rely on a meat thermometer.

In La Donna's day, pasta dishes had two advantages above all others: They were inexpensive, and they were delicious. That's still true today. The weekly household budget can afford an occasional splurge if the splurge is balanced by a little economy. One of her favorite sauces cost little but drew large applause. Moreover, I have learned that if I make too much, the leftover quantity freezes beautifully for the next time.

Italian Sausage Sauce

Coat the bottom of a skillet with olive oil or cooking oil. Skin one-half pound of hot Italian sausages, and brown them slightly. You may leave the sausages whole or chop them into small pieces. Grandmother always chopped them. Add one small onion, chopped, and one green pepper, sliced thinly. Cook the onion and pepper until soft, and add two cups (a one-pound can) of plum tomatoes, chopped or mashed. Season to taste with salt and pepper and a healthy pinch of oregano. Stir well, and simmer the sauce for thirty or forty minutes. If the sauce becomes too thick, add a little hot water to thin it. Serve the sauce over rigatoni or spaghetti.

Grandmothers are expected to provide special treats for visiting grandchildren. That is one of the rules engraved in the universal book of grandparenthood. There is no escaping it—and La Donna never tried. For an exceptionally special treat, she would make her pizza for our lunch.

La Donna's Pizza

Place two cups of flour sifted with a teaspoon of salt in a large mixing bowl, and make a hole in the middle of the flour. In it, place one beaten egg yolk and one-half teaspoon dry yeast dissolved in one-half cup warm water. Beat lightly with a fork, gradually beating in the flour. When most of the flour is mixed in, mix the dough with your hands. Place the dough on a floured board and knead it until smooth. Place the ball of dough in a large mixing bowl that has been sprinkled with flour, cover it with a damp kitchen towel, and allow it to rise in a warm place for a couple of hours or until the dough has doubled in bulk.

Lightly grease a pizza pan, and roll the dough to fit it. Because the dough will be elastic and unwilling to remain rolled out, you will need to pull and stretch the dough until it stays put. Prick the dough in several places with a fork, and brush it with olive oil. Sprinkle evenly over the pizza two ripe tomatoes, peeled and chopped; eight slices of anchovy, chopped; a tablespoon or more of chopped fresh basil leaves; and thin slices of mozzarella cheese or one-half cup of grated Parmesan or Romano cheese. You may add or subtract ingredients. Grandmother sometimes added her own Italian sausage, crumbled and slightly cooked, or thin slices of pepperoni. Dribble a little olive oil over all, and bake in a 400° oven for twenty to twenty-five minutes.

After I grew up and had children of my own, I called my Grandmother periodically for help and advice. She never gave me a recipe in measurements of cups and spoonfuls, but always "some" or "enough," meaning *some* basil and *enough* salt. If I pressed her to be more exact, she would instruct me gently to stir and taste for myself. If the dish tasted right, there was enough seasoning; if it were too watery when stirred, it needed to be cooked longer. How much longer? Some longer. "The way you cook a dish must be your own way, and a dish need not taste precisely the same way another person cooks the same dish. The preferences of your family should dictate the way you cook."

Before she died in 1950, Grandmother gave me her kitchen clock. It had timed all her meals for more than fifty years. It now has regulated my kitchen for more than thirty-five years. Its pleasant tick-tock talks to me of La Donna, and I still can hear her saying, "Never buy anything cheap. You can't afford it."

TWO

My Father, Ben Pietri

My paternal grandfather was a political refugee from Corsica. He found his way to Richmond, Virginia, and settled there. He died before I was born and I never knew him, but I enjoyed the stories my father used to tell me. He told me how Grandpère took over the kitchen every Sunday and prepared a feast for the family, how he made special delicacies for the holidays—candied orange and grapefruit rind, marzipan, and a *bûche de noël.* My father must have helped in the kitchen because he instructed me in some of the same culinary arts.

My father, Ben Pietri, inherited all the French flair. He was a handsome man, small in stature but with a great sense of style; he was also a genius with metals and magnets. More than this, Ben was a naturalist and a conservationist. He enjoyed hunting, but fishing was his passion. We would take walks together in the woods of eastern North Carolina, leisurely strolls, stopping to look at the wildflowers that he knew so well. We picked the beautiful passion flower to take home to Mother, and we found lady slippers that he would not allow me to pick.

I caught my first fish when I was four years old, and from that time on I was my father's fishing companion. He had a special paddle made for me, one smaller than standard, and he taught me to paddle a canoe. He outfitted a small tackle box and taught me to use a fly rod. He had me stand on the back lawn and cast under the weeping willow tree. After I mastered that skill, he made me stand *under* the tree and cast out into the yard without tangling the line in the swaying branches. When I could manage the fly rod to his satisfaction, he took me fishing with him, fly casting from the canoe. We would drift quietly talking in low voices. He identified all the waterfowl. "There goes a wood duck," he would say, when I could see nothing but a dark form against the sky. "Cast beside that log; there should be a bass lurking there." Almost invariably I would get a strike or hook a nice bass.

My father laid down one rule: I had to clean all the fish I caught. Mother expelled us to the back yard for the messy job, and we worked away happily, exclaiming now and then, "The biggest one is mine!" If in truth we had landed a five- or six-pound bass, the beauty was stuffed and baked under my father's supervision.

Baked Bass

Scale the fish, clean out the entrails, and pull out the gills. This job is easily done with a pair of needle-nose pliers. Leave the head and tail intact. Sauté two or three tablespoons of chopped onion and chopped celery in butter or margarine until the onion is soft. Pour the vegetables and butter over one and one-half cups of breadcrumbs; season with salt and pepper and a pinch of thyme. There should be enough butter to moisten the breadcrumb mixture. If the mixture is too dry, add more melted butter. Stuff the cavity of the fish with this dressing. Sew up or pin with poultry pins. Sprinkle the top of the fish with salt and pepper, and place two or three strips of bacon on the fish. Place the fish in a well-buttered baking pan, and bake in a moderate oven, about ten minutes to the pound of fish. The fish is done when it flakes easily when pierced with a fork. Place on a warm platter, garnish with parsley or lemon, and remove the bacon strips.

Those were wonderful days for a small girl who had no playmates. Mother insisted that Father was rearing me like a boy, when I should be treated like a girl, but Father and I were undaunted and inseparable. I believed him to be the font of all wisdom until I was much older and a sophomore in college. It was then that we had glorious arguments over politics.

My father was an excellent cook. He always made the special desserts, cooked the game, garnished the platters, and made the hors d'oeuvres. It was my father who taught me to make pastry.

"Put some flour in a bowl," he said. How much flour? "Until I tell you to stop. Now add some salt and a tablespoon of sugar. Add some shortening." How much shortening? "Until I tell you to stop. With your fingers mix and crumble the shortening into the flour until it feels like coarse corn meal. Use a light touch. Now add ice water, a spoonful at a time, and fluff and mix until the dough begins to stick together. Roll it out gently until it is thin and large enough to fit the pie pan."

Father would let me help him every Christmas when he made ambrosia. Together we would peel the oranges and grapefruit and tangerines and remove all the white membrane from the sections of fruit. Father punched the fresh coconut and drained the milk, which we shared. Then the chore of grating the coconut was shared between us, too. He carefully arranged the ambrosia in a crystal bowl, and sprinkled extra coconut on top. A few maraschino cherries decorated the whole thing.

When I was a child, we lived in Wilson, North Carolina, in the heart of tobacco country. In late summer and early fall the farmers started curing their tobacco in special barns. Fires made of hickory logs were kept burning for a week or so until the tobacco was properly cured and golden brown. The barn was allowed to cool, the tobacco removed, and a fresh batch was carefully placed inside to start the process all over again. The farmers camped out by the barns and kept the fires burning at the proper temperature day and night. Wives and children brought food. At the end of the curing time all the families took turns at preparing a barbecue. They set up long tables near the barns and covered them with food. We feasted on fried chicken, coleslaw, corn on the cob and assorted vegetables, hot biscuits, cakes, and pies. The pork was cooked over a pit lined with hickory coals, and the aroma of the barbecue mixed with the aroma of the cured tobacco could be smelled for miles around.

Because my father was a good friend of most of the farmers of the area, we often were invited to a Saturday barbecue. It was a country party, and the children had more fun than the adults. We played hopscotch, jumped rope, and raced horses, using tobacco sticks for pretend horses. We worked up healthy appetites. The women took care of the food and gossiped while the men turned the spits and basted the pork. My father always helped the men and thus acquired their recipes for the basting sauces. He made barbecued pork for us at home, not over hickory coals, but by roasting the meat in a slow oven.

Two types of barbecue sauce are made in North Carolina. East of Fayetteville the sauce is made of cider vinegar and hot red pepper sauce. No tomato catsup, no sugar, no spices are added. West of Fayetteville the usual tomato sauce is used. My father made the eastern version.

Barbecue

Choose a five- to seven-pound fresh pork shoulder or ham. Remove the skin and most of the fat. Put the pork on a rack in a roasting pan and sprinkle with salt and pepper. Start the roast in a slow oven (275°); after half an hour start basting, and baste every fifteen minutes. Turn the roast three or four times during the roasting process.

Baste with a sauce made of one and one-half cups cider vinegar with one-half cup hot red pepper sauce. Do not use the drippings in the pan. Baste liberally with the sauce, and cook until the meat is very done and ready to pick from the bone. Slice thinly, and serve with coleslaw. The barbecue can be cooked on a spit over hot coals. Use hickory or mesquite chips for your coals.

When I was twelve years old, Father bought me a .410 shotgun. We had many practice sessions at a firing range, and we went skeet shooting. Then I was promoted to a rifle, and after I had learned all the safety rules and had become a fairly good marksman, we went hunting. The perfect morning arrived. We were up before dawn and crept into the woods. Before long, a beautiful doe appeared near us. "Squeeze the trigger," whispered Father. At the moment I had her head in the sight, she turned and looked right at me. Her doleful brown eyes were staring into mine. I burst into tears and dropped the gun. At that moment Father realized I really was a girl, and thereafter he took me fishing.

Father believed that Thanksgiving should be celebrated traditionally. He wanted only wild game for dinner. Mother said it was because he didn't like domestic turkey. Therefore, Father went hunting every November and brought back ducks or geese or maybe a haunch of venison. If all else failed, he would provide squirrels or rabbits. I liked the rabbit best of all.

Many Americans have a strange repugnance towards eating rabbit. Not so in Europe, where the Germans have *Hasenpfeffer*, the Italians have *Coniglio alla Cacciatora* and the French make *Lapin au Vin Rouge*. When Father cooked the meal, we had the French version. When Mother took over the cooking, we had the Italian version.

Lapin au Vin Rouge

Cut a nice rabbit into serving pieces, and shake the pieces in a paper bag with one-quarter cup of flour and enough salt and pepper to season. Brown the rabbit in two tablespoons butter or margarine and two tablespoons olive oil. Remove the rabbit pieces to a three-quart casserole. Cut a large onion into chunks, and scrape six or eight tiny carrots; add the vegetables to the casserole. Pour a cup of Burgundy and a cup of chicken bouillon into the skillet and boil up the liquids, scraping all the brown bits in the pan. Pour the hot liquid over the rabbit, and season with a good pinch of rosemary and a twist of lemon peel. Cover the casserole, and bake in a moderate oven for about an hour and a half or until the meat is tender. Sprinkle the top with chopped chervil or parsley, and serve from the casserole.

Coniglio alla Cacciatora

Brown the rabbit pieces in two tablespoons butter and two tablespoons olive oil. Remove the rabbit to a casserole. In the same skillet, cook one large onion, chopped, until golden. Add five or six anchovy fillets, and mash and stir them until dissolved. Add a cup of tomato purée and a glug of dry white wine (about one-half cup). Add a bay leaf and a couple of sprigs of parsley, chopped. Add salt cautiously, remembering that the anchovies are salty. Add a little more wine if the sauce is too thick. Pour the sauce over the rabbit, cover the casserole, and bake in a moderate oven for about an hour and a half or until the meat is tender. Freeze any leftovers. This dish is even better the second time around.

Dessert for Thanksgiving dinner was invariably sweet potato pie. Father did not like pumpkin, an idiosyncrasy I have inherited. We made the pie together. While I made the crust, Father cooked and mashed the yams, and often we dreamed up ways to vary the recipe a bit.

Sweet Potato Pie

You will need a nine-inch unbaked pie shell, made either from scratch or from any one of the packaged mixes. In a mixing bowl, stir together three-quarters cup of brown sugar, one-half teaspoon salt, one-half teaspoon each of allspice and nutmeg. Add one and one-half cups cooked and mashed yams, two eggs, one and one-half cups thin cream. Beat all together on low speed until the custard mixture is smooth and creamy. Add one or two tablespoons of rum, pour the custard into the pie shell, and bake the pie at 350° for forty or forty-five minutes or until the custard is set. Allow the pie to cool thoroughly, and serve it with a topping of whipped cream.

My father rarely ate desserts, but he did enjoy apple pie. I have used his recipe all these years. The men in the family will consume a whole pie at one meal. If I make two pies, they will have one for breakfast the next day. A word of advice: Use firm, tart apples—Yorks, Staymans, or Winesaps—and go easy on the cinnamon. Too much cinnamon will overpower the flavor of the apples.

Apple Pie

Pare, core, and slice two pounds of tart apples. Sift together three-quarters cup of sugar, one-quarter cup flour, one-quarter teaspoon each of cinnamon, allspice, and nutmeg. Add one-half teaspoon of salt. The salt is important. It heightens the flavor of the apples and cuts the oversweetness of the sugar mixture. Line a nine-inch pie pan with pastry, layer the apple slices and the sugar mixture on the pastry, dot with three generous pats of butter or margarine, and cover with a second crust. Flute the edges of the two crusts and prick the top with a fork. Bake in a medium oven for an hour or until the crust is brown and the filling is bubbly. Serve warm with sharp Cheddar cheese.

When Father was seventy years old, he was forced to retire. He muttered and grumbled about being a useless old man. I was working at the time on a project for Reynolds Metals Company to turn three-by-five sheets of quarter-inch aluminum into pieces of sculpture. I found that hammering the metal into forms was a frustrating job. The aluminum did not respond to my hammering in the expected way. I asked him to visit the studio and explain the stubborn properties of the metal. He did. He was suddenly inspired. He promptly set up a small workshop and started producing sculpture of welded metals. He launched into a new career that brought him twelve years of happiness and some fame.

Before he died, Father gave me his double-barreled .410 shotgun with the advice that we should keep the rabbit population of our home in the mountains under control. I value the gun, but I am more grateful for the culinary skills he left me.

THREE

Green Knoll Farm

It was wartime when Jack and I met. We were young, both working at our first jobs. Jack was a cub reporter on the Richmond *News Leader*. I was finishing work on my degree at the old Richmond Professional Institute of the College of William and Mary, and I was working part-time at a Broad Street store. We met at a museum opening in May, and the inevitable happened. He asked if I would marry him. That was on the Friday after we met on Tuesday. About six weeks later he thought to ask if I could cook. I answered yes to the first question and put off the second. He was not deterred. We were married in September. After a few days' honeymoon, we returned to our tiny apartment on Stuart Avenue in Richmond's West End. The realization dawned on me that we had to eat. I remembered a small family joke about writing a recipe for a new bride: First face the stove. I faced this one. The monster was old and decrepit and very crotchety, and it took several months of coaxing and cajoling before the stove and I came to an understanding. Meanwhile, there were scorched vegetables and burned meats. Grandmother was an invaluable aid, and I pestered her constantly. Gradually I learned to cook by following her instructions and adding a "pinch" of this or "enough" of that.

During World War II, rationing of food was a constant problem for the housewife. Fowl and fish were not rationed and organ meats could be found, but pork, beef, and veal were rationed and often were not available even with the ration stamps necessary to buy them. Butter was scarce and expensive. As a consequence, our menus were limited, but I benefited from Grandmother's advice to save every scrap of food and put it in the stockpot for soup at the end of the week. Every bone and chicken carcass was a prize to be added to the same pot. We ate pasta in every shape and under every sauce. I discovered that beans are a good source of protein.

Those first years were a time of learning and experimenting. Irma Rombauer's *The Joy of Cooking* became my bible. A revised edition can be had in the book stores today, but I refuse to give up my dog-eared copy from 1942. I tried recipes from magazines and newspapers, and little by little I began to make departures that were all my own. I suppose everyone who loves to cook begins in about the same way.

Early in 1944 we had our first son. We moved to a larger flat on West Grace Street. It had high ceilings and drafty floors, and our landlady had one idea of heat while we had another. We wanted out. In fact, we wanted way out, and we began to go exploring on weekends. One Sunday we came across a pre-revolutionary farm house near Glen Allen, not far from the Chickahominy swamp and the Hanover line. It was ten miles from the newspaper office; it was 300 yards from the paved road. It had "great possibilities." Buying it on our income was crazy. We told ourselves that fresh air and pure water and a puppy would be beneficial for our fifteen-month-old toddler. We looked at each other, and we looked at ninety acres of rundown fields and whiskery sedge. And we bought Green Knoll Farm.

It had the main house, with three rooms downstairs, three rooms up, and a rudimentary kitchen attached to the dining room as an afterthought. The kitchen came equipped with an icebox. In the dirt-floored basement was a huge furnace that a previous owner had created by knocking the front out of one furnace and the back out of another. These he had welded together to form a firebox that would take a five-foot oak log. After Jack learned to bank Old Grendel in the morning we stayed warm through most of the coldest winter days. Out back was a two-story barn. Down the hill toward the stream was a swaybacked chickenhouse. Across the stream was a small tenant house. A onetime owner, known around the county as the mad inventor, had invented a machine-gun mount for motorcycles. He used to charge down the hill from the barn toward the creek, spraying spent shells toward the chickenhouse, leaping the stream, and winding up at the tenant house only to reverse the attack.

In any event, we bought the farm. Then we bought a cow. William M. Tuck, governor of Virginia, gave us two New Hampshire pigs. I forgot to say that just downhill from the henhouse was a pigpen maybe six feet by six feet. We put the pigs in the pigpen and they promptly climbed out. It was war from the first moment.

I wanted a garden, so that first spring we had Mr. Meredith, a professional farmer who lived down the road, bring his tractor around and plow about an acre behind the barn. The soil looked like Iowa loam. It was chocolate brown, and it was home to a million earthworms. We were unbelievably naive about things. Neither of us had lived in the country before. So we planted at least a hundred tomato plants. We put in 100-foot rows of beans and squash and corn. Everything grew. Everything grew and grew and grew. Luckily for us, the county then had a cannery a couple of miles away. I went around and canned tons of whole tomatoes and uncounted quart cans of tomato juice. We ate garden produce until we could eat no more. We gave away bushels of vegetables to kindhearted friends who would take the stuff off our hands. The newsroom ate well that summer.

Then there was the cow. We bought it for $50 through a newspaper ad, and had a friend with a pickup truck bring her to Green Knoll Farm. It was a bad start. The cow was not amused by the ride. Furthermore, the cow liked nothing about our poor barn. The cow and I never got along. She was a golden Guernsey, and she gave gallons of milk and quarts of rich cream every day. This cow knew I was afraid of her and she resisted all my efforts to do a friendly job of milking. She kicked over the bucket; she kicked over the stool; she learned how to swat me in the face with her tail; she pushed me to the wall of the barn; and then she belched in derision. She was a hateful cow.

After a couple of months we latched onto an unreliable hired man named William, who professed to know everything about cows and pigs. The idea was that he would live in the tenant house, and in return he would take care of the cow and the two pigs. It worked for a while. I coped with buckets of milk in the kitchen, and William coped with the cow in the barn. (The county agent came around and taught me how to churn. The experience taught me to respect both county agents and store-bought creamery butter. Churning is not for amateurs.) Coping with the amount of cream became a problem. I churned it for butter; we used it on cereal; we poured it on fruit; we whipped it for strawberry and peach shortcakes.

Inevitably some of the cream soured. Then we had sour cream cakes. My sister makes glorious cakes, but she has little success with pies. I make a good pie, but have little success with cakes. However, the Sour Cream Cake never failed to bring raves from guests. One bit of caution: The recipe doesn't work with commercially soured cream. There is not enough butter fat, and the addition of extra butter destroys the texture of the cake.

(*Editor's note*: For an acceptable product using commercial sour cream, increase the cake flour to 2 cups and replace the noncommercial sour cream with 1 [8-ounce] carton commercial sour cream and 1/4 cup whipping cream.)

Sour Cream Cake

Beat two eggs until light; beat in one cup of sugar. Add one teaspoon lemon extract. Stir one-half teaspoon soda into one cup of sour cream. Sift together one and three-quarters cups cake flour, one teaspoon baking powder, and one-half teaspoon salt; add to the egg mixture alternately with the sour cream mixture, beating lightly. Pour the batter thinly into three well-buttered and floured cake pans and bake twenty to twenty-five minutes or until the cake tester comes out clean. Cool the cake and fill between the layers with Cooked Lemon Filling.

Cooked Lemon Filling

Sift together one-quarter cup flour and three-quarters cup sugar, and set aside. Beat one egg slightly and beat in one-quarter cup of lemon juice; add and beat into the sugar-flour mixture. Heat one-half cup of water and the grated rind of half a lemon in the top of a double boiler. Add gradually to egg-sugar mixture, beating until smooth. Return the mixture to the double boiler and cook until thick and no starchy taste remains, stirring constantly. Stir in one-half tablespoon of butter or margarine and cool. Spread between layers of cake.

A simple lemon icing dribbled on top finishes the cake to perfection. I don't remember where this recipe came from. It is written in the back of my old copy of *The Joy of Cooking* in my cryptic handwriting. Someday one of my granddaughters may find it and claim it for her own.

Because none of us in our family is much on desserts, we continued to be overset in sour cream. Thus we hit upon one of the truly magnificent products of American cuisine, the sour cream waffle. The boys always insisted that these waffles actually float. Take them out of the waffle iron, and they propel themselves gently through the air and onto a waiting plate. I have seen sons put away half a dozen of these delicacies, and after a while the sons float. They are the most elegant waffles ever put on a breakfast table. The recipe can be found in Rombauer's original *The Joy of Cooking*.

In time, even though we managed to use the cream, the livestock became more than we could handle. The unreliable William disappeared in a faint miasma of corn whiskey. One afternoon Jack came home from the newspaper to find that the pigs had again done their gypsy caravan through our neighbors' property. He went a mile away, carrying a bucket of corn mash, and came back crying, "Soo-eee, soo-eee," while the pigs danced along behind him, laughing all the way. He got them back in the pighouse, which by this time had been barricaded with cinder blocks and used tires, and he called Mr. Meredith. That good friend came up to our farm with his truck and a couple of two-by-sixes to form a ramp. Mr. Meredith looked these errant pigs in the eye, said "Whup, whup," and the beasts climbed into that truck like five-year-olds into a school bus. Off they went. The cow went next. Then we were down to the chickens.

Jack probably should be writing about the chickens, for he was the one who got us into the ill-fated business. A friend of ours on the *News Leader*'s copy desk had been raised on a farm in Fluvanna County. He professed to know all about raising chickens, and when he discovered that we had a vacant laying house and a repairable brooder house, he sold my innocent husband on a great idea: We would raise eggs for the Pine Top Hatchery. He would give all the advice, and Jack would do all the work. It was our first experience with a consultant. Thus we acquired a flock of Rhode Island Reds. Jack learned to gather eggs from under indignant hens, and I learned to clean and candle the things. We never made a dime on the venture, but during that time we ate like kings.

I will say this for those chickens: They produced. We kept all the double-yolk eggs for our own consumption. We had plenty of broilers at just the right weight. There was an extra dividend. Chicken feed in those days came in colorful designer cotton bags. I made cup towels, aprons, and kitchen curtains out of those feed bags. Whenever Jack had to buy feed, I told him what pattern we needed to complete the set of napkins. When the baby chicks grew up we culled the flock. The young roosters were fattened and taken to market to be sold as fryers. The rest were grown for layers. I insisted on holding back two dozen of the roosters and fattening them on corn and grain until they weighed in at four pounds. We dressed them out and froze them for our own use. They were plump and tender and juicy. Of course, we never wasted any of the chicken. When we had roast chicken, I saved the carcass and used it for Brunswick stew or gumbo. If we had fried chicken, I withheld the backs and wings and used those parts for soup or gumbo.

Chicken Gumbo

Break up the chicken carcass, and put it in a soup pot. Cover it with water, and add salt to taste. Simmer until the meat comes from the bones. Cool the broth somewhat, and remove all the bones. Replace the meat in the stock, and add one large onion, chopped; a couple of stalks of celery, chopped; and four or five tomatoes, peeled and chopped. Use canned tomatoes if good fresh ones are not available. Add one package of frozen baby lima beans and one package of frozen okra. Cover the pot, and simmer for thirty or forty minutes. Add one package of frozen corn and a tablespoon of Worcestershire sauce. Taste for seasoning. You may want to add a couple of shakes of Tabasco sauce to spice it up a bit. Simmer an additional ten minutes, and serve. The soup should be thick, not watery. The recipe works equally well with leftover turkey.

Chicken or Turkey Curry

In two tablespoons of butter or margarine, sauté one onion, chopped, and one apple, peeled, cored, and chopped, until they are soft. Mash the apple and sprinkle with one tablespoon of flour and one tablespoon curry powder, stirring the onion, apple, and flour well together. Add one and one-half cups of chicken bouillon, and stir until smooth. Taste for seasoning, and add salt if needed. Add two cups chopped cooked chicken or turkey. Simmer the curry for ten or fifteen minutes, stirring once or twice. Add one-half cup of cream, and stir well. Serve the curry over hot cooked rice.

Along with the curry, serve a condiment tray of chutney, chopped nuts, grated coconut, raisins plumped in brandy, chopped hard boiled eggs, minced green pepper, or whatever might please you. The more condiments, the better.

During the Green Knoll years, as long as the chicken passion lasted, we fairly gorged on chicken. We had Southern fried chicken. We had roasted chicken. I called on Grandmother for help, and she came through gloriously with her *Pollo alla Cacciatora*. It remains a family favorite.

Chicken Cacciatora

Cut a chicken into serving pieces, and brown in one-quarter cup of olive oil. Use a large skillet with a top. Push the chicken aside (or remove it), and add one small onion, minced; one stalk of celery, minced; and one green pepper, minced. Cook and stir until the onion is soft and golden. Add one can of Italian tomatoes, mashed; a good pinch of rosemary; and a crushed clove of garlic. Salt and pepper to taste. Replace the chicken, and add a glug of dry white wine—about one-quarter cup. Cover the skillet, and simmer for thirty-five to forty minutes. Stir periodically, and add a little more wine if the sauce becomes too dry. Serve with spinach noodles, and spoon some of the sauce over the noodles.

There is a French variation of Chicken Cacciatora. The recipe for this dish comes with a delightful tale. After the Battle of Marengo, it is said, Napoleon's chef, Dunan, found himself with nothing to serve the general for dinner. He liberated a chicken from a nearby farm, commandeered a few fresh tomatoes, and found wild mushrooms to help his cause along. Wine was a staple. *Et voilà*! A classic was born.

Poulet Marengo

Heat two tablespoons of butter or margarine and two tablespoons olive oil in a large skillet. Cut up a young chicken in serving pieces, and allow them to brown slightly in the skillet. Remove the chicken pieces to a three- or four-quart casserole. Add one chopped onion and one-fourth pound sliced mushrooms to the skillet and allow them to brown slightly. Sprinkle with two tablespoons flour. Stir well and moisten with one-half to three-fourths cup of dry white wine. A domestic chablis is as good as the more expensive imported French variety. Add two tablespoons of tomato paste, salt and pepper, and stir until the sauce is smooth and somewhat thickened. The sauce should have the consistency of thick cream. If it is too thick, add a bit more wine. Pour the sauce over the chicken, cover the casserole, and bake in a moderate oven for forty-five minutes or so. If guests are late, the chicken will hold in a warm oven for another twenty or thirty minutes. Freeze any leftovers. The dish is better the second time around.

All good things come to an end, and so our years at Green Knoll Farm came to an end. We look back on those years with an affection we did not always feel at the time—not when Jack was changing two flat tires a day, not when he was repairing the Rife ram pump in the middle of a January night, not when he was mucking out the broiler house, not when I was cleaning eggs, not when I was feeding heavy logs to Old Grendel, not when I was at the cannery over a steaming vat of tomatoes, and certainly not when I was trying to milk that cow and churn the butter. But we had two sons and a third on the way, and they would need a little better education than Henrico County could provide in those days. Jack was about to be made editor of his newspaper, and his job would demand more time in the city and less in the henhouse. We sold our beloved Green Knoll Farm, shed some tears, and moved into the city.

FOUR

RICHMOND

Toward the end of 1951, after three years of living in the West End suburbs, we came to a decision: We ought to live all the way in the country, or all the way in the city, but we were not meant for the in-betweens. By good fortune we found an Edwardian townhouse on Hanover Avenue in the Fan District of Richmond. It was twenty-four feet wide, but it was half a block long, and the high-ceilinged rooms were hooked together like boxcars. We added closets and extra bathrooms, hung colorful wallpaper, and put on coats of fresh paint.

At the very back of the townhouse was a large kitchen overlooking a small garden. We paved the garden with old bricks, built a six-foot brick wall, added a fountain, and erected a wrought iron pergola with a copper roof. We left borders for planting camellias with fringes of parsley, and I planted a glorious rosemary bush in the sunniest spot in the garden. The townhouse was far removed from the ninety acres we had roamed at Green Knoll Farm, but we came to love city life as dearly.

Our three sons cheerfully made the transition to city life. They could walk to school and to the city library. They could catch a bus on Saturday mornings and go to the movies. They made friends—dozens of friends, hungry friends—and they constantly brought their friends home and into my kitchen. They came for snacks after school, and with little notice or no notice at all, they often stayed for dinner. When I asked our eldest, Sean, why he and his brothers seemed never to eat anywhere else, he said they didn't like the food anywhere else. It was a lovely compliment. The boys grew, and their appetites grew with them. The cookie jar appeared to have a hole in the bottom. Gallons of ice cream disappeared from the freezer. There never was enough peanut butter. But, after all, these were male children. They would construct mile-high sandwiches, running over with pickles and relishes, and still eat three healthy meals a day.

These were busy years. A nearby carriage house became available, and I snatched it up, turned it into a sculptor's studio, and returned to my own profession. We entertained. Jack brought visiting newspapermen home for dinner. During sessions of the Virginia General Assembly, state legislators often lingered over after-dinner coffee to talk of pending bills. Hungry artists found their way to our table. Meanwhile I was maintaining a full schedule of work in the studio, teaching three classes a week, giving lectures, judging art exhibits, and serving as a member of the Virginia State Art Commission.

Schedules had to be maintained and food budgets kept in line. I found it helpful to write up the menus for the week and to do the major marketing only once a week—a regimen I still follow. We had invested in a small freezer that saved both time and money. Like my grandmother before me, I found a butcher in Richmond's old market area and waited for his specials on meats. We bought a hind quarter of beef or a whole lamb, and I stood in the sawdust beside the butcher while he cut the meat to my specifications. I found that I could conserve time by preparing casseroles in advance. These could be frozen or refrigerated and heated at dinner time. The boys, out to tease, had a label for anything in a casserole: glup. It was disconcerting when they referred to an aromatic *boeuf Bourguignon* as "glup."

Dinner was always a family get-together. I insisted on linen napkins, candlelight, and no reading at the table. We tried to promote interesting and civilized conversation, but there was a certain amount of hilarity, too, especially when the boys tried to out-pun their father. The four males had a game they played when no guests were present. I established a firm rule: The catsup bottle positively will *not* appear at the dinner table! Rule Two was that no catsup whatever could be added to dishes prepared with herbs and wine. They often managed to sneak the offending bottle into the dining room and secrete it under the table. When a casserole appeared, they would ask: "Herbs and wine?" If I sighed and said "No," the catsup was passed under the table from son to son and son to father. I tried not to look. Boys will be boys.

Sunday dinner usually was the important meal of the week. I had time to spend in the kitchen and would prepare a leg of lamb or a rib roast or a stuffed chicken or turkey. The roast gave us three meals. The second time around we had stew if it were beef, curry if it were lamb, or chicken tetrazzini if it were poultry. The bones and scraps of meat then went into a soup pot. Our soups were hearty meals in themselves, usually served on Saturday nights in cold weather. A steaming bowl of thick vegetable soup or gumbo, accompanied by thick slices of French or Italian bread, made a nourishing meal. The boys, fearing imminent starvation, also wanted a dessert—a hefty cobbler or an apple pie to fill the cavities that remained.

One of our favorite soups was *Pasta e Fagiole*. It is a Neapolitan soup, rich in proteins and vitamins, inexpensive to put together. After a Saturday afternoon football game, the boys and their friends lapped it up. The recipe came from my grandmother. You won't find it in a cookbook for gourmets.

Pasta e Fagiole

Soak overnight one pound of dry navy beans, following the package directions. The following morning start the soup pot with four quarts of water, some beef bones, a ham bone, or a good-sized ham hock. Bring the water to a boil and add the beans; a two-pound can of stewed tomatoes; one large onion, minced; and a clove of garlic, crushed. Add salt to taste. Simmer the beans, stirring frequently, until the beans are tender. Remove the bones from the soup, and taste the soup for seasoning.

At this point, you may cool the soup and let it rest in the refrigerator. The flavors will be improved. An hour or so before serving time, gently heat the soup.

Cook one-half pound of shell or elbow macaroni *al dente*, drain it, and add it to the soup. Ladle the soup into large bowls and sprinkle Parmesan cheese on top.

Feeding three growing sons was no easy task. The boys required quantities of food—sheer volume was their aim—but they could be finicky also. The youngest son disliked turnips and nuts. The middle son, to his father's mystification and distress, wouldn't touch black-eyed peas. They all enjoyed oysters, Maine lobster, soft-shell crabs, curries, and many out-of-the-ordinary dishes. For everyday meals they got along with less exotic fare. The casseroles and glup, which were varied and frequent, turned ordinary food into more appealing fare. By itself, cabbage is an uninteresting vegetable, but I cooked it with pork chops in a casserole. We usually served baked beans and a tossed salad with the casserole. The boys were well fed.

Casserole of Pork Chops and Cabbage

Choose a one-half-inch-thick chop per person to be served. Trim all fat from the chops, and gently brown them in a skillet sprayed with a vegetable cooking spray. Do not cook them through. Remove the chops to a four-quart casserole. Pour one-half to three-quarters cup of water into the skillet and boil it up, scraping up all the nice brown bits.

Meanwhile, quarter a small head of cabbage, and remove the core. Place the cabbage on top of the chops, and pour the sauce from the skillet over all. Season with salt and pepper and a pinch of savory. Cover and bake it in a medium oven for thirty to forty minutes. The cabbage will steam and absorb the flavors of the pork without loss of vitamins.

Dishes of pasta have been a mainstay in our household. We eat ground beef and elbow macaroni, salmon en casserole, macaroni baked with sliced tomatoes and sour cream—the list is long. Leftover chicken or turkey usually ends in Chicken Tetrazzini.

Chicken Tetrazzini

Cook one-quarter pound of sliced mushrooms in three tablespoons of butter and an equal amount of olive oil until the mushrooms give up liquid. Sprinkle with two tablespoons flour, and blend. Pour in one cup of chicken broth and one-half cup of dry white wine. Stir and cook until the sauce thickens. Add one-half cup of diced cooked chicken or turkey. Meanwhile, cook one-half pound of very thin spaghetti *al dente*. Drain the spaghetti well, and place it in a well-buttered rectangular baking dish. Pour the chicken mixture over the spaghetti, and sprinkle the top of the casserole liberally with Parmesan cheese. Bake in a moderate oven for about fifteen minutes, or until the casserole is hot and bubbly.

Our salmon casserole evolved one day when I was rushed for time and the refrigerator was bare. The pantry yielded a can of salmon and a can of cream of mushroom soup. I found a package of tiny green peas in the freezer. Plenty of pasta and a jug of dry white wine always were on hand. I gave the casserole a French name and served it without apologies. The men asked for seconds.

Saumon au Vin Blanc et Champignons

Drain the liquid from a one-pound can of pink salmon, and save the liquid. Remove the dark skin and bones, and flake the salmon. Cook one package of frozen green peas until just barely tender, and drain them. Put one can of cream of mushroom soup, undiluted, in a saucepan. Pour the salmon liquid in the can, and add enough dry white wine to half-fill the can. Add one tablespoon dry dill leaves. Heat the soup and liquids, stirring until all is smooth.

Meanwhile, cook one-half pound of elbow macaroni *al dente*, drain it, and put it in a two-quart casserole. Mix together the salmon, peas, and sauce, and mix thoroughly with the macaroni. Sprinkle the top with breadcrumbs and snipped parsley, and bake in a moderate oven until hot and bubbly.

All families have traditions, and some of the happiest ones have to do with traditional foods on holidays. I inherited some from my family, and we started some traditions of our own. I find now that the wives of our sons are carrying on some of our traditions while making some of their own.

Our Thanksgiving feast never varied from year to year. We had the usual turkey, candied yams, and tiny green peas or green beans, but we also had an oyster casserole and apple pie. The turkey was stuffed with a bread and giblet dressing and basted with white wine and butter. The boys and their father ate it with gusto, and they all fought amicably for the last oyster in the casserole. To this day we have an oyster casserole every Thanksgiving, and the three sons insist on serving it at their own holiday dinners.

The oyster recipe was told to me by a friend who grew up in Williamsburg. It never has been written down, and I have had my daughters-in-law stand by me in the kitchen while I prepare it so that they, too, can carry on the tradition. Nice plump, juicy Chesapeake Bay oysters should be used. I have tried Pacific Coast oysters, Maine oysters, and oysters from the South Carolina coast, and I have wound up with failures.

Oysters Marie

Melt a stick of butter in a large skillet. Seed and finely chop one large green pepper, and sauté it gently in the butter until the pepper is soft. Pour a quart of oysters into a colander over a bowl, and drain as much liquid as possible from the oysters, reserving the liquid. Sprinkle about one-third cup of flour over the butter and green pepper mixture in the skillet, stirring all the while. If all the butter has not been absorbed by the flour, add more flour. Stir and cook on moderate heat for several minutes. Add two tablespoons

Worcestershire sauce, one teaspoon lemon juice, and one-half teaspoon of hot pepper sauce. Add salt to taste. Stir in the oyster liquid, and stir and cook until there is a thick paste-like sauce. Remove the skillet from the fire, and with a wooden spoon gently mix in the oysters. When the oysters have become well coated with the sauce, pour them into a buttered two-quart casserole. Sprinkle the top with breadcrumbs, about one-third cup, and bake the casserole uncovered in a moderate oven for thirty minutes. The casserole should be hot and bubbly and the oysters plump and juicy. Do not overcook.

Christmas in the city was a gala affair. Richmond has a great tradition of decorating doorways for the Christmas season. Many homeowners in the Fan Disrict put gas lamps on the sidewalks. December twilights were moments of beauty. Our boys started two weeks before Christmas preparing for the holiday. They made excursions into the country looking for a tree and for a bird's nest to put in it. They made havoc in the kitchen baking cookies. On the Sunday before Christmas the boys were allowed to invite their friends to a tree decorating party. When the tree was finished and approved, the teenagers tuned their guitars and recorders and gathered around the piano for carols. The house rang out with joyful noises. In the process, the young people worked up healthy appetites. There was usually a large pot of chili con carne on the stove, and the round oak table in the kitchen we spread with dips and potato chips and a big bowl filled with mixed raw vegetable salad. Everything vanished, leaving barely a cookie crumb behind.

Christmas Eve was joyful. We started with a dinner of spaghetti with Grandmother's sausage and tomato sauce, and afterwards we hung stockings on the mantel in the front parlor. Everyone bundled up for the twenty-mile drive to our little country church in Goochland County for midnight service. The drive back home was never subdued. The boys and their father, filled with the Christmas spirit, sang lustily in four-part disharmony.

After all the presents were opened Christmas morning, we had a festive brunch of sour cream waffles, sausages, and Italian eggs.

Italian Scrambled Eggs

Melt three tablespoons butter in a large skillet, and gently sauté five or six spring onions or scallions that have been chopped. Use as much of the green tops as possible. Add a one-pound can of tomatoes, chopped and drained; a good pinch of basil; and salt and pepper. Let the tomatoes cook down until no liquid is left. Beat eight eggs with one-quarter cup of light cream. Pour the eggs in the skillet with the onions and tomatoes, and stir constantly until the eggs are cooked but not dry. Turn out on a platter, and sprinkle with fresh snipped parsley.

Christmas dinner was always a cold buffet. The boys wanted to be free to visit their friends, and family members and neighbors came and went. The cook of the household refused to spend the holiday in the kitchen. In the afternoon the sideboard became our groaning board, covered with a shimmery *Boeuf en Daube*, sliced baked ham, marinated vegetables, potato salad, homemade pickles and relishes, and the traditional fruitcake. Family and friends served themselves whenever they were hungry.

Boeuf en Daube

Trim a four-pound rump roast of all fat. Pour a couple of tablespoons of olive oil in a heavy iron pot or Dutch oven, and heat the oil. Sear the roast on all sides. Add one large onion, chopped, and three or four whole carrots, scraped. Remove the pot from the fire and add one split pig's foot. Season with salt and pepper and a bouquet garni. Pour in a mixture of two-thirds dry white wine and one-third water, so that the beef bathes well therein. Cover and bake slowly for three or four hours. Taste for seasoning. The beef should be tender but not stringy.

Let the beef cool in the liquid. Remove the beef and slice it nicely and arrange it in a deep platter. Slice the carrots and garnish the platter with them. Chill the platter of beef. Skim the fat from the sauce, discard the pig's foot, and strain the sauce. Chill the sauce until syrupy; then glaze the beef with sauce and chill until firm. Allow the remaining sauce to gel completely; then whip it with a fork and decorate the edges of the platter with the gelatin and sprigs of fresh parsley.

The daube keeps beautifully for several days in the refrigerator. Some French recipes call for a calf's knuckle, but this is impossible to find in American markets; I have found, however, that the pig's foot gives off abundant gelatin and somewhat improves the flavor of the dish.

When Sean went off to The University, as the University of Virginia in Charlottesville *always* is identified, he swiftly became disenchanted with the food served in the student cafeteria. He convinced three of his friends that four young men could rent a small house, do their own cooking, and live better and more cheaply than they could live in a university dormitory. This decision led to a crash course in cooking and marketing between his freshman and sophomore years. Sean brought his typewriter into the kitchen. Before long he accumulated an impressive stack of file cards that gave him recipes for most of our everyday meals. I took him on my weekly marketing trips. He learned to choose tender meats by examining their fat, and to choose vegetables that had not been too long in the warehouse. He learned to cook, as I had learned, with "a pinch of herbs" and a "piece of butter the size of a walnut." In the kitchen with me, he chopped and minced and stirred and tasted. He basted and mixed. After three months of tutelage he learned to cook quite well—so well that his housemates all gained ten pounds the first semester. He had also learned to feed four healthy young men on a limited budget. One of their favorite meals was Meat Loaf and Corn Soufflé.

Meat Loaf

Put in a blender one onion, one carrot, and one stalk of celery, all coarsely chopped. Add one egg and half of a six-ounce can of tomato sauce. Blend until nicely mixed. Mix this with one pound lean ground beef and one-half cup of breadcrumbs. Add salt and pepper and a good pinch of dried bouquet garni. Mix all well together, and pat into a loaf shape. Place the loaf in a rectangular baking dish, not a loaf pan, that has been sprayed with vegetable cooking spray. Pour a little water in the pan, only enough to cover the bottom. Bake in a moderate oven for thirty minutes. Add a tablespoon of Worcestershire sauce and a little chopped fresh or dried parsley to the half can of tomato sauce you have left. Pour over the meat loaf, and bake an additional fifteen minutes.

The corn soufflé will bake along with the meat loaf. They both take the same amount of time at the same oven temperature.

Corn Soufflé

Spray a soufflé dish or deep casserole with vegetable cooking spray. Beat together a one-pound can of crushed (cream-style) corn, two egg yolks, and one-half cup of thin cream. Beat two egg whites until stiff, and fold into the corn mixture. Pour mixture into the soufflé dish, and sprinkle the top with paprika. Bake at 350° for forty-five minutes or until the soufflé is brown on top and no longer runny.

Our small walled garden in back of the townhouse proved to be a charming spot for small dinner parties in the summer. We covered card tables with pink or green linen tablecloths, lit dozens of candles, and spread a table under the pergola with a cold buffet. The fountain bubbled in the background. The three sons—for a modest fee—tended bar, cleared plates, and served the dessert.

Twenty years later, after Jack had resigned his editorship to write his column from Washington, we were seated at a dinner with former Governor and Mrs. Albertis Harrison. She recalled having dinner in our garden, and even requested the recipe for the jellied chicken I had served.

Poulet Marie

Poach four chicken breasts, boned, halved, and skinned, in one cup of chicken stock (it can be made with a chicken bouillon cube) and one-half cup dry white wine. Season with salt, if needed (remembering that the chicken bouillon cubes are salty), a dash of onion powder, and a pinch of tarragon.

Simmer the chicken gently for twenty minutes or until tender, and let it cool in the stock. Remove the chicken from the stock, and chill thoroughly. Strain the stock through two thicknesses of cheesecloth and add one envelope of gelatin softened in one-quarter cup of water. Heat and stir until the gelatin dissolves. Cool somewhat, and add two tablespoons of mayonnaise. Chill the stock until it is syrupy. Coat the chicken with this mixture and chill again. Decorate with sliced black olives and fresh tarragon (or parsley or watercress); coat again with gelatin. Refrigerate four or five hours. Serve on a chilled platter, and garnish with cocktail tomatoes and parsley or watercress.

The boys grew up on Hanover Avenue. They played stickball in the alleys of the Fan District, learned to come home by the chimes of St. James, fell in love, fell out of love, learned to drive. In time, Sean was graduated from The University, Chris joined the Navy, and Kevin went off to boarding school. Toward the end of 1966, when Jack's syndicated column had begun to catch on, it became apparent that the time had come to go. We shed tears at leaving our beloved house on Hanover Avenue, with all the friends and family who had shared it with us, but we found a big new house in Old Town Alexandria and launched into another chapter.

FIVE

White Walnut Hill

When the boys had outgrown summer camp, we began searching for a small piece of property in the Blue Ridge Mountains of Virginia. It took a long time, but in January of 1966 we found a small farm in Rappahannock County. It was love at first sight. Here we would be blessed with magnificent views, with complete privacy, with pure and constant spring water—and also with thick red clay soil and absolutely intractable rocks. The thirty-five acres were bounded on the south by a small stream known on old maps as White Walnut Run. We promptly named the place White Walnut Hill. A white walnut, for the record, is the same thing as a butternut tree. Our teenaged sons spent happy weekends roaming the countryside. In the early summer they picked blackberries for cobblers; in the fall they went hunting for rabbits and squirrels. They fished in nearby ponds and visited newfound friends from neighboring farms. We renovated a small cottage, demolished an awesome four-hole privy, put in central heat, and installed a working kitchen. The cottage could then be used year round. Early in 1967 we left Richmond.

To give Jack a base in Washington, we acquired a large townhouse on Princess Street in Old Town Alexandria. It is the pleasantest place to live in the whole of the capital area, and we developed a real affection for the old streets and picturesque houses of this unpretentious city. Even so, we had an abiding love for the beauty and peace of White Walnut Hill. For that reason, the decision was made to build our dream house at the farm. Another two years passed before the house was completed and the basic landscaping was done.

Our first attempts at gardening were like a granddaughter's first try at a three-layered devil's food cake. These were, alas, a limited success. The space planned for vegetables was on a slope, there being no flat ground in Rappahannock County; consequently, the lettuce and spinach seeds washed down the hillside during spring rains, and the tomatoes and beans withered in the heat of July.

We decided that a garden in the European fashion might work, and we proceeded to lay out a terraced plot. We fenced the area to keep out the rabbits and groundhogs, but this barricade also proved a limited success. The rabbits climbed over the fence and the groundhogs tunneled under it. We planted dwarf apple and pear trees to be espaliered to the fence, and we laid out boxes six feet by twelve feet with grass paths in between. The boxes, formed of four-by-fours, worked splendidly. There is something about a sixty-foot row that dampens the gardening spirit, but ten six-foot rows inspire an early-morning vigor.

We started a compost pile. Who can say enough for compost? In these hardscrabble hills, compost is the gardener's salvation. We have majestic oak and maple and hickory trees. In the autumn we rake all the leaves and feed them into a gasoline-fired grinder nicknamed the Gloppity-Glop Machine. We traipse through the pastures, bearing shovels and green plastic bags, and we collect those magnificent meadow muffins so providently left by the cattle. Some of our neighbors regard these quests as a little bit odd, but the natural manure hastens and enriches the decomposition of the leaves. Throughout the year we save all vegetable matter from the kitchen—the potato peelings, grapefruit rinds, celery tops, crab shells, moldy bread, and spoiled milk—and these too are carefully buried in the compost pile.

By spring we have compost as beautiful, in its way, as the odes of Keats and the arias of Verdi. This is the compost of kings—rich, black, squirming with earthworms. We dig it into the planting boxes, and now, after fifteen years, the gooey clay has become friable soil. When the tender young seedlings peek up in the spring, we mulch them thickly with more compost. Over the growing season there are almost no weeds, and it is unnecessary to cultivate. The soil stays moist and cool, and if a weed has the audacity to appear, it is easily plucked by hand. Planting in well-prepared boxes means planting the vegetables more closely, and because pollination is more effectively achieved, we get excellent yields.

We grow only those vegetables we particularly like. In a typical season we plant four varieties of lettuce, half in early spring and half in the fall. We plant spring and fall spinach also, and we always manage to eat the whole crop raw in salads. Baby lima beans, green beans, and black-eyed peas are regulars in our garden. An asparagus plot produces bountifully. We plant four varieties of tomatoes. Other boxes hold cucumbers, squash, and cantaloupes. Some boxes are edged with onions and radishes. Red and green peppers do handsomely. We grow midget eggplant in two wooden tubs outside the back door where they can be constantly watched for bugs and can be easily watered when we refill Happy's water bucket.

We had to have an herb garden. By good fortune, a long strip of rocky, gravelly area next to the parking area proved a perfect spot. It was sunny; the drainage was good, and it was close to the kitchen. There we planted parsley, chervil, tarragon, savory, oregano, chives, and dill. We worked in whole wheelbarrows of compost to loosen the soil, and every summer we mulch the plot with cocoa bean husks. The garden looks pretty and it smells like Hershey bars. Herbs love the rocky soil and full sunlight, and they thrive. It's one of the many pleasures of country living to slip out to the garden to snip chives for scrambled eggs, or to cut sprigs of parsley to garnish a fish.

Over the years we have learned to garden by trial and error. (Jack says it is my trials and his errors.) One year I planted carrots as a border in front of the cucumbers. My housemate, in one of his especially helpful humors, pulled them all up. He thought they were Queen Anne's lace. The following year, in his eagerness to share the burdens of cultivation, he carefully weeded the spinach. When he was finished, I found a great crop of lamb's quarter. I once left it to him to plant the black-eyed peas. It seemed only fitting. He picked up the wrong package of seeds, and when his black-eyed peas came up, they were lima beans.

We find that we can save most of our produce for winter by freezing the vegetables, and by putting up pickles, relishes, and jellies. Excess vegetables go into the soup pot for gumbos and soups. I make quantities of tomato sauce and freeze it. In August, when pots of chutney and chili sauce are bubbling on the stove, the kitchen smells of heavenly spices. The packed jars form a stained-glass window in the pantry.

There are times when the garden produces too much of a good thing. One summer we tried a new variety of squash. The seed catalog had extolled its virtues in rhapsodic prose. Thus hooked, we planted one of the six-by-twelve boxes in Kuta squash, and spent the rest of the summer hacking away at lush vines that threatened to blanket the county. Those seeds produced squash the size of country hams.

Cucumbers also tend to get out of hand. We grow cucumbers in wire cages about eighteen inches wide and four feet tall. The system allows us to plant more hills than we otherwise could plant, and because the cucumbers grow upward, it's easier to pick them. Ordinarily we get such bumper crops that visitors and family members are pressed to take bags of cucumbers home with them. We eat cucumbers in sour cream flavored with fresh dill leaves; we slice them into mixed salads; we peel, seed, and stuff the large ones with chicken or tuna salad; and we make pickles—Kosher dills and curry pickles. The curry pickles are especially good with cold lamb, and they make an interesting addition to the condiment tray when serving lamb or chicken curry.

Curry Pickles

Do not peel, but slice thinly twenty-four small cucumbers. Put the cucumbers in a large bowl, and add one-half cup of salt and two quarts of water. Let the cucumbers stand for four or five hours. I do this part of the job just before bedtime and let them stand overnight. Drain and rinse the cucumbers well, and drain again. Combine three cups vinegar, two teaspoons curry powder, one and one-half cups sugar, one teaspoon dry mustard, and one tablespoon celery seeds in an enamel pot, and bring to a full boil. Add the cucumbers, and heat just to the boiling point. Pack into hot sterilized pint jars and seal. There should be seven or eight pints of pickles.

One of the most popular dishes I concoct in the summer is a cucumber aspic. When weekend guests are expected, I usually make it a day in advance. It beautifully graces a cold buffet, and it is a delightful complement to cold poached salmon.

Cucumber Aspic

Peel and chop three or four medium cucumbers, and put them in the blender with a couple of sprigs of parsley and fresh dill leaves. Use a scant tablespoon of dried dill leaves if you don't grow your own. Soften three envelopes of plain gelatin in one cup chicken bouillon, and then heat the bouillon, stirring constantly, until the gelatin dissolves. Add this to the cucumbers and blend until puréed. Add salt and ground white pepper to taste, and chill the purée until syrupy. Fold in one and one-half cups of sour cream and one-quarter cup of mayonnaise; pour all into a lightly oiled mold, and chill until firm. Unmold on a chilled plate, and garnish with cucumber slices and cocktail tomatoes. *Note*: If you're using bouillon cubes, remember that the bouillon will be salty, so you may not need to add salt. Taste to be sure.

For a few years we had a running argument here at the farm. Jack wanted a swimming pool. I wanted a hothouse. We compromised: We built a covered heated pool where he could exercise all year round, and at the southern end of the pool house we provided potting benches and a sink for me. Just before Christmas the seed catalogs arrive in the mail, and we spend the week between holidays poring over them all. Every year we test a different vegetable, but generally we stick with the varieties that have done well in the past. In January the packets of seeds, the peat pots, and the special potting soils arrive. In mid-March I clear and scrub the benches and start flats of tomatoes, eggplants, and peppers. In mid-April we plant seeds of cucumbers and cantaloupe directly into large peat pots and give them a good head start before they go into the garden. In this way we can grow the varieties we prefer, and we get larger, sturdier plants than ordinarily we could get from local nurseries. Besides, it's more fun to do it ourselves.

Sixteen tomato vines provide about all the tomatoes we can cope with. They begin producing in early July, and they keep going until frost in October. I make gallons of sauce for pasta and freeze it. We feast on cold sliced tomatoes sprinkled with fresh basil. We stuff whole ones with shrimp salad. One favorite dish calls for baked tomatoes with herbed crumb topping. Everyone seems to like a casserole of stewed tomatoes. It goes especially well with a fresh-caught largemouth bass from son Sean's pond.

Oven Stewed Tomatoes

Skin and coarsely chop four or five large ripe tomatoes. Mix with the tomatoes two stalks celery, chopped; add two or three scallions, chopped, or one-quarter cup of snipped chives, and mix. Place the vegetables in a casserole with a pat of butter the size of a walnut and a couple of tablespoons of chopped fresh basil. Mix in a cup of croutons and salt and pepper to taste. Bake at 350° thirty or forty minutes, and sprinkle the top with Parmesan cheese. If you find this dish too acetic for your taste, add one grated carrot to the tomatoes. Carrots have a natural sugar which melds flavors without adding calories.

In the summer we often have Sunday brunch on the deck, where we can rest our eyes on the mountains and watch the bluebirds. Charlie, the chirping sparrow, usually joins us at his special feeder. Overhead is a canopy formed by a giant chestnut oak. Squirrels go steeple-chasing down the fence, leaping over the bluebird boxes, and chipmunks raise their tails and challenge our snoozing Shetland sheepdog. It's a peaceful time, a lazy, restful way to spend a Sunday morning. There is time to dawdle over coffee and the Sunday papers. We visit the garden early and pick several large red ripe tomatoes, about the size of baseballs, and we cut a few sprigs of chives. Then we have eggs baked in tomatoes with tiny sausages and rolls or croissants.

Baked Eggs in Tomatoes

Core, seed, and drain four or more large tomatoes. Butter generously a shallow casserole or baking dish, and place the tomatoes in the dish. Break an egg into each tomato, being careful to keep the eggs whole. Sprinkle the tops with snipped chives and salt and pepper. Bake in a moderate oven for thirty minutes or until the eggs are cooked to your liking. We like ours fairly soft.

We grow black-eyed peas every year for two reasons. The man of the house loves them, and the peas make an excellent soil builder. They lock in a good deal of nitrogen and provide a natural fertilizer. At the end of the season the dead pea vines are carefully chopped up and added to the compost pile.

What is the proper way to cook black-eyed peas? Southerners have fought duels on the issue. One faction holds that the peas should be cooked with a ham hock and served with stewed tomatoes on the side. An opposing faction insists on cooking the peas and tomatoes together. My father refused to eat black-eyed peas at all. He contended they were good only for pigs. I had to call on my grandmother for help. She provided me with her Italian version. We pick the peas when the pods are well filled and still green. Jack takes over the job of shelling them, a task he has perfected after many years of practice. We gather a basket of really ripe tomatoes.

Black-Eyed Peas and Stewed Tomatoes

Skin four plump tomatoes and quarter them or roughly chop them. In a good heavy pot (enamel over iron is my choice), melt a piece of butter the size of a walnut, and add one small onion, finely chopped. Stir and cook until the onion is golden; then add the chopped tomatoes. Add one-half teaspoon of dried savory and salt and pepper. Add a little water if the tomatoes are not juicy. Cover the pot, and simmer the tomatoes for twenty or thirty minutes. Add about two cups of shelled peas. If fresh ones are not available, the frozen ones will do almost as well. If there is not enough liquid to just cover the peas, add more water. Cover the pot, and simmer until the peas are soft but not mushy—about twenty minutes. Frozen ones will take a little longer than fresh ones. Serve with baked ham and cornbread.

We are a family that eats salads—tossed green salads, seafood salads, chefs' salads. On hot muggy nights we have cold dinners of turkey or chicken salad with marinated green beans, tomatoes, and fresh asparagus. We have aspics. We have potato and pasta salads. My list is long.

No salad is good without a good dressing. Some years ago I took a cruise on a French ship. Most of the passengers were French. A group of Americans sat at the table next to ours. On the second night at sea a passenger at the next table asked our waiter for French dressing on his salad. Our waiter tried to explain that the dressing was of course French, but the passenger insisted he wanted *real* French dressing. "You know, it is pink and it comes in a bottle." The waiter disappeared and conferred with the salad chef who came from the galley and in his most polite way explained in French that he knew not how to make a salad dressing that was pink and came from a bottle. So few Americans know that there are innumerable French dressings, but the one most used for mixed salads is a sauce vinaigrette.

Sauce Vinaigrette

To one-third cup of good wine vinegar, either red or white, add two-thirds cup virgin olive oil. Season with a little salt and freshly ground pepper. To this basic sauce may be added herbs—basil, tarragon, thyme, savory. One also may add capers, Roquefort or blue cheese, minced anchovies, or dry mustard. Do not add sugar.

On those sultry summer days when appetites droop, it is pleasant to have something cold and pretty for dinner. We usually wait until the sun has set behind the mountains, and then we have supper on the deck. There we get a bass viol serenade from the bullfrogs in the pond below the hill. A platter of Salmon Mousse garnished with thickly sliced tomatoes and marinated cucumbers perks up the appetite.

Salmon Mousse

Soften three envelopes unflavored gelatin in one-half cup of bottled clam juice and dissolve the gelatin in one cup boiling clam juice. Drain two one-pound cans of pink salmon and remove the bones and skin. Place the gelatin mixture and salmon in a blender with three sprigs fresh dill leaves or one-half teaspoon dried dill. Blend until pink and frothy. You may have to blend only half at a time because the whole batch doesn't fit into the blender. Pour the salmon into a bowl, and add one-quarter cup mayonnaise and one-quarter cup sour cream; whip up until thoroughly mixed. Chill until syrupy. Decorate a lightly oiled fish mold with olives, pimiento, and parsley. Pour in the salmon mixture, and chill until firm. Unmold on a chilled platter, and garnish the platter. Serve a bowl of Green Mayonnaise with the mousse.

Green Mayonnaise

Green Mayonnaise is simple to make and is a lovely dressing for cold fish and especially salmon. It is indispensable for whole salmon in aspic. There is no hard and fast rule on ingredients, but only fresh herbs can be used. Chop one-half cup of mixed green herbs—parsley, tarragon, dill, chives, and a couple of blanched spinach leaves. The spinach is not really necessary; it only heightens the color. Put the herbs in a blender with two or three tablespoons of mayonnaise, and blend until the herbs are thoroughly puréed. Mix the purée into two cups of good mayonnaise. I use more chives than parsley and far more dill than tarragon. If the spinach is young and very tender, it is unnecessary to blanch it.

Our two tubs of eggplant, flanking the back door like a pair of Chinese lions, produce so much produce that we serve eggplant in all kinds of ways. Once in Sicily we learned to love pasta served with an eggplant sauce. It has become one of our favorite meals. I make large batches of sauce when the eggplant and tomatoes are ripe. It freezes nicely and is low in calories and cholesterol.

Spaghetti alla Siracusa

Heat one-half cup of olive oil in a large skillet, add two or three sliced cloves of garlic, and sauté until the garlic is brown. Remove and discard the garlic. Add one medium eggplant that has been peeled and cubed and one green pepper that has been seeded and chopped. Cook over medium heat, stirring periodically, until the eggplant is soft. Add three or four slices of anchovies; cook and stir until the anchovies dissolve. Add three cups of fresh tomatoes, skinned and chopped, or the equivalent of canned tomatoes. Season with salt and pepper and a generous pinch of oregano. Simmer for twenty minutes or so, and add one-half cup of sliced black olives and a tablespoon of capers. Simmer an additional ten or fifteen minutes, and taste for seasoning. If the sauce is too thick, add a little hot water. There should be enough sauce for one pound of spaghetti. Pass a bowl of grated Romano cheese, the true imported cheese made of goats' milk. This sauce is one that begs for the flavor of a robust cheese such as Romano.

I believe that fresh, tender vegetables are so good they should be cooked and served as simply as possible. This is a rule I abide by when cooking eggplant.

Baked Eggplant

One small eggplant is sufficient for two people. Wash the eggplant, remove the stem, and slice the eggplant in two lengthwise. Score the meat sides half an inch or so deep. Place the eggplant halves in a baking dish with just enough water to cover the bottom of the dish. Dribble olive oil over the eggplant, and sprinkle the halves with garlic salt and fresh snipped basil or the dried variety. Bake in a moderate oven until the eggplant is soft. It will take about thirty minutes. We like it served with cold roast lamb and sliced tomatoes.

One year we received a free packet of Sugar Daddy, which Park Seed Company introduced as "the world's first stringless snap pea." The peas were planted; they thrived; they produced great quantities of peas until a drought dried them up in July. We picked and ate those peas right off the vine in the garden. We tossed them raw into mixed salads. We cooked them, too. No one in our household cares especially for stir-fried vegetables. We're not much on steaming vegetables either, for steaming often diminishes the flavor. However, I tried an old French recipe for baking green peas and discovered that the flavor and crispness of the snap peas could be retained when they're cooked by this method.

French Style Peas

Wash the peas and drain them. Line a shallow casserole with washed lettuce leaves, leaving them somewhat wet. Use Bibb lettuce, not iceberg. Put the peas on the lettuce and add only a sprinkle of salt. Add two or more pats of butter depending on the amount of peas to be cooked. Do *not* add water. Cover the casserole and bake in a moderate oven ten to fifteen minutes. Test them after ten minutes for doneness to your liking. This can be cooked on top of the stove, but the pot must be watched carefully or the lettuce will scorch.

We keep a careful garden journal in which I record which vegetables have been planted in which boxes. We list the varieties planted, and I make notes on how well each variety has produced. Did we have a bad time with insects? Did fungus hit the squash? We keep track of droughts and frosts, and we now have a fifteen-year diary of the garden.

Early in our gardening days Jack announced that the fresh vegetables were wonderfully good, and they certainly were a convenience, but wouldn't it be more economical just to buy fresh vegetables from local markets? To prove him wrong, I kept records of outlays for seeds, potting materials, and dried cow manure, our only extra fertilizer. After every picking I daily weighed the vegetables and checked current prices. I charged off our labor to recreation and exercise. That year we picked twenty-seven pounds of green beans, forty-two pounds of squash, enough cucumbers to make twenty-eight quarts of pickles, and whole bushels of lima beans and black-eyed peas. After two weeks of picking tomatoes, I gave up following the procedure of weighing the baskets we brought in every day. The freezer filled with frozen vegetables and soups, and the pickle cabinet filled to overflowing. We had indeed saved money.

We plant a garden now for the sheer pleasure of watching the seedlings sprout, grow to maturity, and produce beautiful fruits that truly do look like pictures in the Burpee's catalog. We plant a garden because the fresh-picked vegetables have a flavor and goodness that can't be bought. We plant a garden because it is a religious experience for us. We recognize the wondrous design of a Supreme Being in every little seed we tuck into the earth.

Yet I confess that we are not only reverent, but also superstitious. We try to plant by the phases of the moon. Root crops we plant on the moon's wane, all other crops on the rise. I still repeat a very old English ditty as I place the seeds in a row:

> One for the rook, one for the crow,
> One to die, and one to grow.

SIX

Parties and Luncheons

White Walnut Hill has proved to be a lovely place to have a party. The house will accommodate up to thirty guests for dinner, and the deck and back lawn will hold as many as one hundred and fifty.

Starting in the summer of 1972, we began hosting an annual Fourth Estate Field Day for newspaper and TV friends from Washington and Virginia. Actually there are no athletic contests. These were called off in 1973, so we explain, after the javelin team from the *Washington Post* elected to receive. We erect a colorful orange and white striped tent between the house and gardens, and set up two long tables to hold the food. The deck is turned into a bar where guests help themselves to drinkables.

Many of our guests bring tennis gear and bathing suits. They come early and stay late, and they consume great quantities of food. The menu never varies. We put out platters of fried chicken and baked ham, big bowls of macaroni salad, and trays of fresh tomatoes, cucumbers, pickles, and relishes. The dessert always is the most sought-after item. I scoop out a large watermelon, decorate the two halves, and fill them with a spiked fruit compote. Guests sit on the lawn in the shade of our huge chestnut oak and revel in the fresh air and the beauty of the mountains.

The logistics of feeding one hundred and fifty guests out of a family kitchen are formidable, which is one of the reasons for sticking to the same menu. Starting on Wednesday before the Saturday party, each day's activities are carefully planned and orchestrated. On Wednesday, Hilda Alther and I go to the supermarket. Hilda came to work for us in 1970 and has been our indispensable housekeeper ever since. We pick up the chickens and the two preordered Virginia hams. The hams have been precooked and need only to be baked and flavored. Thursday we bake the hams; Friday morning we make the macaroni salad; Friday night after dinner we mobilize all the sons and wives and grandchildren who happen to be around. They fall to work peeling and chopping fruit for the compote. On Saturday morning Hilda oven-fries the chicken, and everything all comes together for a picnic lunch at two o'clock.

Macaroni Salad

It is impossible and unnecessary to give exact measurements. For four servings, cook one-half pound elbow macaroni *al dente*. Drain the pasta and dump it into a large mixing bowl. Immediately, while the pasta is still very hot, dribble over it enough vinaigrette dressing (see Sauce Vinaigrette, page 48) to coat. Mix carefully with a wooden spoon and make sure there is enough dressing to keep the pasta from sticking together. To pasta mixture, add chopped celery, chopped scallions, chopped green or black olives, and chopped pimiento. Season with salt and pepper to taste, and add a good pinch of oregano or dill. Let the salad cool somewhat; then add a tablespoon or two of good mayonnaise. Chill and garnish with pimiento and olives or peeled chopped tomatoes.

Pimientos

Take six or more sweet red peppers, wash them, and place them on an oiled cookie sheet. Bake them in a slow oven (275°) for about thirty minutes or until they deflate and shrivel a little. Cool the peppers until they can be handled comfortably, and peel off the skin. Use your fingers for this job. Wash out the seeds and discard the stems. Slice the peppers into strips, place the strips in a plastic container, and dribble olive oil over them. They are now ready to use. (Pimientos will freeze well, but if they are to be frozen, they should be put in small containers and frozen immediately. In this event, do not add olive oil.)

Baked Ham

Remove the skin and most of the fat from a precooked ham. If you like, score the fat side and stud with cloves. Bake the ham in a slow oven (300°) for about two hours (or fifteen minutes to the pound). Baste the ham at twenty- or thirty-minute intervals with a good Burgundy or Madeira. Be cautious with the Madeira, for the alcohol content is high and may cause the ham to flame up.

Fruit Compote

Our luncheon dessert always gets compliments. One large watermelon will provide two shells for containers and a wealth of melon balls. We mix melon balls from four honeydews and eight cantaloupes. Then we add six pints of blueberries and six pints of strawberries; four or five cans of pitted Queen Anne cherries, drained; five cans of pineapple bits, drained; four large cans of mandarin oranges, also drained. Pour in one pint of kirsch. Mix all tenderly together and let steep overnight. Scoop out the watermelon halves, scallop the edges, and upend them to drain well. Fill with fruit just before serving, and garnish with fresh mint. This recipe will feed one hundred guests, but you will have to refill the watermelon shells.

When all our friends of the media have finally drifted away we cope with the leftovers, if there are any. Leftover chicken goes into chicken salad for Sunday's lunch, and the scraps and bits of ham make jellied ham mousse for later in the week. The ham bones go into the soup pot for *Pasta e Fagiole*. Grandmother's law, "Never be wasteful in the kitchen," is carefully obeyed.

The annual press parties are our largest efforts at entertaining, but they have not been quite as memorable as one party we gave late in May of 1981. That one we will never forget. It began with a passing thought at the dinner table some time in February. Jack had met Ronald Reagan when he was covering the Republican convention of 1964, and they had corresponded off and on over the years. Their friendship deepened during the campaigns of 1976 and 1980, and now, early in 1981 we had an idea: Why not invite the newly elected president and Mrs. Reagan for a small luncheon? It might be a welcome change for them from the formality of state dinners at the White House.

We extended an invitation through the proper White House channels, but heard nothing until Jack spoke with press secretary Jim Brady at the Gridiron Club's dinner on March 28. "I think you've got the Prez," Jim whispered. Two days later, leaving the Washington Hilton hotel, Mr. Reagan was gravely wounded by an assassin's bullet, and Jim Brady was nearly killed. Of course, we abandoned the whole idea, but the invitation still was in the active file at the White House.

The first week in May, things began to happen. A team of telephone engineers arrived at the farm to check on the lines coming into our central box in the garage. I inquired about this curious visit, and was told only that a request for the information had come from "the president of A.T.&T." This somehow seemed unlikely. A few days later the mystery was cleared up. The White House called to say that Mrs. Reagan and the president, now fully recovered, would be delighted to come. And would we please provide immediately a list of our guests, with their dates of birth and Social Security numbers. Consternation!

We had three weeks to put together the guest list, send the invitations, plan a menu, manicure the grounds, clean the rugs and draperies, check the linens, and polish the silver. We had agreed there would be only twenty for the luncheon—a number I could handle easily.

One week before the party, four young men from the Army Signal Corps arrived in a large truck. They took over the kitchen of our guest house and turned it into headquarters for a worldwide communications system. They ran wires here and there. They erected antennae. They installed extra telephones in the main house, including a telephone for Mrs. Reagan. Shortly afterward the Secret Service arrived to set up security precautions, to decide where the helicopters would land, to arrange for local ambulance and fire protection, and to see how our quiet country road could be guarded.

A contingent from the Secret Service arrived to sweep the house for bombs. They tromped through the two attics with a trained sniffing dog, a well-behaved Labrador who was all business; they crawled under the house; they inspected every room, every closet, every drawer and cupboard. Meanwhile, Hilda and I were busy in the kitchen preparing food, washing crystal, and ironing napkins. We were still thinking in terms of lunch for twenty.

It was about then that I was told there would be two helicopters. The second would hold ten aides who always accompanied the president. They would need to be fed. In addition, at least one platoon would show up from the White House press corps. I began to count: We were now feeding seventy.

During the week, the four Signal Corps specialists got bored. They had a switchboard that could handle fifty incoming calls, but nothing much was coming in. They popped into the house one by one to ask if they could help in any way. I was in the process of preparing a whole salmon in aspic, a process that takes three days. Moving the fish from a refrigerator in the storeroom to a work counter in the kitchen, in order to apply the several layers of aspic, became something of a chore. I willingly enlisted their help. At once they christened the salmon The Whale and cheerfully carried it back and forth for me.

In the course of our conversations, I mentioned that we had two sons in service, one assigned to the U.S. embassy in Abidjan, the other serving on a destroyer somewhere in the Mediterranean. Their modest boast was that they could reach any telephone in the world in fifty-five seconds. To demonstrate their equipment, they put through a call to Kevin's apartment in Abidjan. It was the middle of the night in the Ivory Coast. Kevin sleepily answered the ring, to be brought to full wakefulness by a message: "The White House is calling." He fumbled for a response. "Wait till I put on my pants," he said.

The day of the luncheon arrived. We woke up to grey skies and a gentle misty rain. The house was spotless. At eight o'clock came a knock on the front door. It was the bomb squad, back again. They went through the entire inspection one more time, with Hilda trotting after them, mop in hand. They had a little action. In the attic over our bedrooms, the black Lab stopped before Kevin's old army footlocker and barked, or whined, or said something—whatever sniffing dogs do—and a screwdriver had to be provided to pry the lock open. The footlocker contained a pair of tennis socks. The team departed.

All systems were go. The sun came out at noon. The guests were due at one o'clock. At 12:15, would you believe it, the bomb squad appeared *again*. They wanted to make one more sweep. Little Vesuvius erupted. All five feet, ninety pounds of infuriated woman stood before four burly men, one impassive woman agent in a jumpsuit, and one increasingly disappointed dog. I ordered them to the back door where they could take off their muddy shoes and towel off their dog. My next vision was of five towering security agents, sock-footed, tiptoeing in single file through the house. The young woman was carrying the dog.

All our guests showed up on time. The helicopters fluttered in. Our local volunteer fire department dramatically stood by with foam and hoses at the ready. And the luncheon went smoothly. The menu was not elaborate. In addition to the salmon, we served a molded rice salad, a platter of vegetables marinated in vinaigrette dressing, tiny corn muffins, and fresh strawberry tarts. We served a dry white Italian table wine with lunch and domestic champagne with dessert. Over in the guest cottage, the White House aides got roast beef. Down at the tenant house at the foot of the hill, the press corps got potato salad, cold cuts, and beer.

Saumon en Gelée

In a fish poacher, make a court bouillon of two cups of dry white wine, two cups of fish stock (bottled clam juice works well), one tablespoon of salt, six or eight peppercorns, green celery tops, two medium onions that are quartered, two carrots that are sliced, a sprig of thyme, and four or more sprigs of parsley. Simmer for thirty minutes; then lower the whole salmon on its rack into the poacher. If there is not enough liquid to cover the fish, add water. Turn down the heat and simmer the fish gently until it flakes when pierced with a fork. It will take five to seven minutes to the pound. Let the salmon cool in the liquid; then remove the salmon to a board or platter. Remove the skin and dark meat from the uppermost side. Turn the fish, and remove the rest of the skin and dark meat. With the back side of the fish facing you, carefully remove the central backbone. You will need to use your fingers for this job. The bone should slip out whole without pulling the fish apart. Next, chill the fish.

Clarify the court bouillon by adding one egg white and one crushed egg shell. Bring the bouillon to a boil; strain through two thicknesses of cheesecloth. Measure the amount of liquid and dissolve the right amount of plain gelatin—one envelope of gelatin to one cup of liquid—in the hot stock. Chill the stock until it is slightly syrupy, and brush one coat of aspic on the chilled fish. Let this aspic coating gel; then decorate the fish with fanciful shapes of cucumber, hard-cooked eggs, watercress, lemon slices, pimientos, or whatever appeals. Coat the fish again with aspic and chill thoroughly. Coat the salmon with aspic twice more. Allow the remaining aspic to gel, whip it with a fork, and garnish the edges of the fish platter. Put a cherry tomato in the mouth of the fish and chill until you are ready to serve. Serve this lovely creation with a sauceboat of Green Mayonnaise. (For recipe, see page 49.)

Molded Rice Salad

To four cups of hot cooked rice, add one and one-half cups cooked green peas, one-quarter cup minced green onions, and one-quarter cup minced, drained pimientos. Add enough herbed vinaigrette sauce (see Sauce Vinaigrette, page 48) to coat the rice and to season it well, but be sparing. Mix gently and pack into a lightly oiled mold. Chill overnight and turn out on a chilled platter. Garnish with cocktail tomatoes, watercress or parsley, and sliced or quartered boiled eggs, green olives, or whatever else appeals.

Marinated Vegetables

On a large oblong platter, arrange rows of cooked crisp tender vegetables that have been separately marinated in a sauce vinaigrette. (You may have a favorite recipe, or try mine on page 48.) Green beans, lima beans, tiny whole beets, artichoke hearts, cauliflower florets, broccoli florets, tiny whole carrots, tiny whole potatoes or potato balls—whatever you like. Add savory and a hint of garlic to the sauce when marinating the bean family; use parsley or chervil for potatoes, and marjoram and garlic for broccoli and cauliflower. Chill the platter for several hours.

Our guests rose from the table about 2:30, but President and Mrs. Reagan weren't ready to go. We had some conversation about the elaborate communications facilities over at the guest house, and Jack had mentioned the boast of the Signal Corps specialists that they could reach any telephone in the world in under fifty-five seconds. The president was amused and amazed. "Well," he said, grinning, "let's see about that."

He took daughter-in-law Gina by the hand and headed for the cottage. The specialists snapped to attention. A three-star general, arms akimbo, stood in the doorway to watch his men at work. The president explained that Gina's husband was a quartermaster on the destroyer *Pratt* somewhere in the Mediterranean. Here was a challenge. Sure enough, breaking through the chatter of ships at sea, the call flashed halfway around the world. It took a little doing, for the fleet was on maneuvers, and the general in the doorway kept getting impatient. But at last—after considerably more than fifty-five seconds, the commanding officer heard an unforgettable message. The president of the United States wanted to speak to Christopher Kilpatrick. Son Christopher, who happened to be loafing on the stern at that moment, was hustled to the bridge. The president said he had someone at his elbow who wanted to speak to him. "I miss you," said Gina. That was about the size of it. Christopher later wrote the president that it was like God calling the Vatican to ask for an altar boy.

SEVEN

CHARLESTON

I cannot recall when we first fell in love with Charleston. It must have been some time in the late 1950s or early 1960s, and it may have been at a gathering of editors. We stayed in the old hotel on the Battery, and I had an opportunity to walk through the old part of the city. Other Southern cities have great charm—New Orleans, Mobile, or Savannah—but every subsequent visit to Charleston strengthened our original attachment to that city. The more we visited, the more we wanted to return.

One thing led to another. Son Christopher was assigned to a destroyer squadron based in Charleston. We kept making visits. The idea took root that it might be nice for us to buy a house in Charleston, partly as a good investment, and partly to provide a warm and comfortable spot in which I could avoid the winters of Rappahannock County. The Blue Ridge Mountains are idyllic all year round, but in January they can get the least bit bleak.

Thus we acquired a big old house—a typical Charleston house, long and narrow and lined with piazzas down the east side. It is a before-the-earthquake house, meaning that it was built before the city was shaken by the earthquake of 1886. The tremor gave the house a remarkable tilt. We noticed that the east side of the kitchen is six inches lower than the west side, but it had other charms. A white picket fence enclosed a large corner yard. Palmettos and lovely old crepe myrtles shaded the lawn. We carved out wide borders along the fence for plantings of azaleas, camellias, and gardenias. We laid a brick patio in back and set aside a small plot for plantings of herbs, lettuce, peppers, and tomatoes and plunged into the life of the "Holy City."

Old Charleston is a small city built on a peninsula formed by the confluence of the Cooper and Ashley rivers. (The standing joke, which all newcomers are required to admire, is that the Cooper and the Ashley come together at Charleston to form the Atlantic Ocean.) It is a gracious small town. It is still an active port and boasts an old and imposing Customs House. Such features as the Battery and Rainbow Row are well known. Most of the original houses are intact and meticulously maintained. Charlestonians are proud of their heritage and guard against any destruction of the charm and flavor of their city. A board of architectural review has been established, and no homeowner in the historic district can alter the exterior of a building without its approval.

Gardens are an important element of the city. Flowers and shrubbery bloom all year long, and garden and house tours abound. The loveliest affair is a candlelight tour that is held in April and again in October. A walk through the city should be punctuated by pauses to peep through cast-iron gates. Dozens of cameo gardens are tucked along the sides of the old houses. Camellias start blooming in December and January, and gerberas follow in riotous profusion. Often the paper white narcissus blooms for Christmas. In early March we hang baskets of ferns and geraniums on the piazzas and do a bit of elevated gardening. Azaleas burst into full, glorious bloom in April, and tourists pack the large public gardens. August is the dead month when most of the inhabitants leave the city and escape both the heat and the mosquitoes.

The cultural season opens in September and extends through the final explosion of the Spoleto Festival in June. Charlestonians enthusiastically support drama, opera, ballet, and symphony. Children get acquainted with the arts in kindergarten and learn to appreciate culture while they are acquiring social graces.

Our nearby supermarket is indeed super. One can find fresh seafood of all kinds and special cuts of veal and lamb. The produce section overflows with fresh vegetables and fruits. In late January or early February we get the tiny fresh asparagus, known locally as chaney briar, and often fresh snow peas are laid out beside eggplant and green beans. All the ingredients for my European dishes are at hand, and I am often inspired to plunge into my tiny kitchen and cook up specialties for the grandchildren.

Like my grandmother before me, I believe that small children should have nourishing foods, and periodically the oldest granddaughter, Alina, is invited for dinner. Her favorite meal is baby loin lamb chops, rice with mushrooms, and tiny green peas. The lamb chops are simple and quick to prepare.

Broiled Lamb Chops

Rub both sides of each chop with a cut clove of garlic, salt them lightly, and sprinkle them with basil, fresh or dried. Broil the chops until they are brown but still pink inside. The lamb chops should be juicy and succulent.

The sailor of the family likes lamb chops baked in a casserole that can be prepared in advance and put in the oven thirty or forty minutes before dinner. Use the less expensive shoulder chops. They will cook slowly in a sauce and will become more tender in the process.

Baked Lamb Chops in White Wine

Rub six shoulder lamb chops, well trimmed of fat, with garlic, salt, and pepper, and brown them in three tablespoons of butter or margarine. Transfer the chops to a casserole. Sauté in the same skillet one-quarter pound of sliced mushrooms and three or four chopped green onions and their green tops. When they are soft, stir in one and one-half tablespoons of flour, blending well. Gradually add one generous cup of dry white wine and cook until the sauce thickens, stirring constantly. Add two healthy pinches of basil and salt to taste. Pour the sauce over the lamb chops, cover the casserole, and bake in a moderate oven for thirty minutes or until the chops are tender. If the sauce thickens too much, add a little more wine. The sauce should have the consistency of thick cream.

Serve this delectable dish with wild rice for a special treat. Green beans or snow peas are a nice accompaniment. There is an alternative method for baking lamb chops in wine sauce that is quick and easy and best saved for busy days.

Baked Lamb Chops—Alternative Method

Brown the chops and green onions as in the preceding recipe. Transfer them to a casserole. Pour into the skillet one can of cream of mushroom soup diluted with *half* a can of dry white wine. Stir over heat until the soup is smooth and add the pinches of basil. You may not need additional salt because the soup is already well salted. Pour the soup over the chops, and proceed as above.

The fresh seafood in our Charleston market is both varied and beautiful. A shopper will find red snapper, fresh cod, sea bass, flounder, shrimp, crabs, clams, and oysters, even squid. They provide the makings for the seafood dinners we enjoy. We feast on Shrimp Creole, *Flounder à la Bonne Femme*, and *Zuppa di Pesce*, as well as other seafood dishes.

Tomato and Shrimp Aspic

Soften two envelopes of unflavored gelatin in one-half cup cold V-8 juice, and dissolve it in three and one-half cups very hot V-8 juice. Cool the juice/gelatin mixture and chill until syrupy. Finely chop one stalk of celery and add to the gelatin mixture, along with two tablespoons minced fresh parsley and one tablespoon minced fresh dill. Add one-half pound of tiny cooked shrimp. Mix all ingredients thoroughly, pour into a ring mold, and chill until firm. Unmold the aspic on a chilled platter, and fill the center with cottage cheese that has been flavored with one or two tablespoons of grated onion and one tablespoon of Worcestershire sauce.

Bernice's Crab Casserole

Sauté three or four small green onions and their green tops, finely chopped, and half a green pepper, finely chopped, in two tablespoons of butter or margarine. When the vegetables are soft, mix them and the butter they were cooked in with one pound of crabmeat and two or three heaping tablespoons mayonnaise. Add two or three tablespoons snipped parsley and a dash or two of hot pepper sauce. Place the crab mixture in a casserole, sprinkle the top with breadcrumbs, and bake in a moderate oven until casserole is bubbly.

There are as many recipes for shrimp creole as there are New Orleans cooks, and there is no exact method for preparing the dish. Basically, there is a spicy tomato sauce to which the shrimp are added and the whole mélange is served over rice. I have found that fresh tomatoes make the best sauce and I often make up double portions and freeze half for winter meals.

Shrimp Creole

Cook one pound of fresh or quick frozen shrimp in salted water until the shrimp turn pink. Shell and devein the shrimp if necessary, and set aside. Save the shrimp stock. Heat two tablespoons bacon drippings in a large skillet and sauté one onion, chopped; one stalk of celery with leaves, chopped; and one green pepper, chopped. Stir and cook until the vegetables are soft. Sprinkle one tablespoon of flour over the vegetables and cook, stirring constantly, until the flour takes on color. Add four large tomatoes, skinned and chopped; a pinch of thyme; one-half teaspoon of hot pepper sauce; salt and pepper. Add one cup of shrimp stock, and stir until the sauce is smooth. Simmer the sauce until the vegetables are very soft, about thirty minutes. If the sauce thickens too much, add a little more stock, but don't let the sauce get soupy. Add the cooked shrimp, and simmer an additional five minutes. Taste for seasoning, and add more hot pepper sauce if you like hot, spicy foods. Serve over rice.

Some years ago, we spent a winter vacation in Taormina, Sicily. The ancient town is perched on top of a mountain and overlooks the sea far below. From our hotel, we delighted in a magnificent view of Mount Etna. It was puffing out plumes of white smoke while we were there. We trudged up and down the narrow cobblestoned streets; we visited the ruins of a Greek theatre; we shopped for antiques. When fatigue and hunger overtook us, we popped into any one of several *trattorias* for lunch. The Sicilian cuisine is a mixture of Greek and Italian styles. The island produces an abundance of vegetables and fruit, as well as excellent full-bodied wines. Fresh seafood comes from the surrounding seas. It was in Taormina that we tasted our first *Zuppa di Pesce*—a fish stew not very different from the French *bouillabaisse*.

In Charleston we can find seafood somewhat like the Mediterranean varieties, and a pot of fish soup often simmers, waiting for the sailor of the family to come home for his favorite meal.

Zuppa di Pesce

Pour four or five tablespoons of olive oil into a heavy stockpot or soup pot. Brown two cloves of garlic in the oil, and then discard the garlic. Sauté one finely chopped onion in the garlic oil until the onion is transparent, and add a one-pound can of chopped plum tomatoes, juice and all. Add one-half cup of dry white wine and a good pinch of thyme and salt and pepper. Cover the pot and simmer for about thirty minutes. You will need three or four pounds of assorted fish fillets—sea bass, fresh cod, red snapper, perch, or whatever firm fleshed fish may be available. (Do not use American sole or flounder. These fish cook into a disagreeable mush.) You also will need an assortment of shell fish—half a dozen little neck or cherrystone clams, half a dozen mussels or small oysters, half a pound or more of shrimp (either fresh or frozen), and if you like, one small squid, thoroughly cleaned, washed, and sliced.

Scrub the clams and steam them in a separate pot; remove them from their shells and strain the juices through a sieve lined with paper towels. Add the clam juice to the soup pot, but set the clams aside. If you use mussels, treat them the same way. Add the sliced squid to the soup; cover and simmer fifteen or twenty minutes or until the squid is tender and easily pierced with a fork. Add the fish fillets (cut into two- or three-inch chunks) and simmer another ten minutes. Now add the cleaned shrimp, clams and mussels, and/or raw oysters to the mixture; simmer until the shrimp are pink and the oysters curl.

Serve this aromatic soup in large soup plates and pass thick slices of Italian or French bread that has been toasted with garlic butter. In Sicily it is proper to dip the bread in the soup.

Granddaughter Alina did not like fish, and her parents hesitated to force her to eat a food she disliked. Gina, her mother, appealed to me for a recipe that might appeal to the child. Because Alina was entranced by her French classes, we agreed to try a French recipe. We told Alina she would learn a few more words to add to her vocabulary, and she could explain the dish in her class. She agreed. She ate the fish and to our delight exclaimed, "*Je l'aime*!"

Poisson à la Bonne Femme

Cover the bottom of a flat baking dish or an oblong Pyrex dish with melted butter or margarine. Sauté a quarter of a pound of mushrooms, and sprinkle them evenly on the bottom of the baking dish. Chop four or five green onions with some of their green tops, and sprinkle them over the mushrooms. Layer one pound of fish fillets—red snapper, flounder, or fresh cod—on top of the vegetables. Salt the fish, and sprinkle with a couple of pinches of thyme. Dot the fillets with butter, and add a dry white wine, just enough barely to cover the vegetables. Do not let the fish swim in wine. Bake in a moderate oven, basting two or three times, until the fish flakes easily. It will take no more than ten to fifteen minutes, depending on the thickness of the fillets. Carefully remove the fish to a warm platter; add one tablespoon of *beurre manié** to the wine vegetable sauce in the baking dish; stir until smooth, and return it to the oven for about five minutes or until the sauce thickens nicely. Pour the sauce over the fish and add a sprinkling of chopped parsley.

**Beurre Manié*: Cream together about one tablespoon softened butter and one or two teaspoons flour. Add mixture to the liquid that is to be thickened; bring just to a boil, but do not boil.

We can buy veal in Charleston. It is always a treat we can't resist. Our favorite dinner is *Osso Bucco* served with spinach noodles and a mixed vegetable salad. Alina's little sister, Charlotte, eats it with gusto and then demands, "More osbuc, peese." The dish is made with veal shanks simmered in a tomato sauce. In some areas of the country, the butcher will cut the shanks for customers. Sometimes one can find them already cut and packaged in the meat department of some supermarkets.

Osso Bucco

Have the butcher saw the shanks into one-inch pieces. You will need one or two pieces per serving. Sprinkle them lightly with flour. Heat four or five tablespoons olive oil in a large skillet, and brown two cloves of garlic in the oil. Remove and discard the garlic. Brown the veal shanks in the hot oil. Remove the shanks. Add one onion, sliced thinly; one carrot, grated; one stalk of celery, chopped. Stir and cook the vegetables for about five minutes. Add one pound of canned plum tomatoes, a pinch of marjoram, a pinch of rosemary, salt, and pepper. Let the tomatoes simmer for a few minutes, and then add one-half cup of dry white wine. Replace the veal in the skillet, cover it, and simmer for about an hour. The veal should be very tender. Check it periodically, and add more wine if the sauce becomes dry. Serve with fresh snipped parsley. Add green noodles to each plate, and spoon the sauce over all.

We look forward to many more years of visits to Charleston. We anticipate the cries of joy from our three granddaughters. We enjoy the walks around Colonial Lake, stopping to watch the sea gulls and pelicans. It is rewarding to stand by when Alina mixes up a batch of cookies.

If my five beloved granddaughters grow up with a healthy respect for food and the preparation of it, then I shall have left them wealth indeed.

EIGHT

From the Recipe File

Four decades of cooking have taught me a few dos and don'ts, and have led to some recipes that didn't seem to fit into the preceding chapters. One of the things I *do* is to use herbs and spices. One of the *don'ts* is not to use them with a heavy hand.

A long time ago—I think it may have been as a speaker before a women's club—I had an assignment to talk about herbs. It proved a pleasant task. The use of herbs for medicinal purposes probably goes back to prehistoric times. We know from written records that Egyptian doctors were using herbs 2,000 years ago in the treatment of patients. Both the Old and New Testaments make repeated references to herbs. Aristotle let us know that he had a garden of more than 300 plants. The Romans were devoted to herbs in both cooking and healing, and the monks in Christian monasteries carried on the practice. It helped, of course, that so many of our favorite herbs grew wild in the Mediterranean area.

A story I especially liked was of Napoleon. He said that he could smell his homeland island of Corsica before he could see it because the scents of rosemary, thyme, marjoram, and lavender wafted across the sea.

When New Orleans was settled, French housewives relied upon ships from Europe to bring herbs, but sometimes the ships disappointed them. They appealed to native Indians and learned to use chile peppers and ground sassafras leaves, known as filé. A distinctive regional cuisine was born. Across the continent our English forebears were discovering other native herbs. Thomas Jefferson had a large herb garden. It has been reconstructed for the benefit of tourists who visit Monticello.

In my own family the tradition of culinary herbs is firmly established. My specially designed herb shelves hold fifty herbs and spices, and in the garden border near the back door we grow the herbs we use most often. Two medicinal plants always are kept nearby—aloe for burns and jewelweed for poison ivy. The jewelweed grows wild near the springs at the bottom of the hill. It's always handy—and sad to say, every summer it's always needed.

Parsley is more than a simple garnish in our kitchen. Many years ago I learned from a Polish doctor that parsley is an excellent palliative for stomach ulcers. We chop parsley into green salads, add it to sauces and fish dishes, and nibble on it for indigestion. We consume a lot of parsley.

A word about sage: It is the most overused herb in America. Whole generations of cooks have grown up believing that sage must be added to the turkey or chicken dressing. Sage is a strong herb. It easily can overpower a dish. We grow it in the herb garden because it smells nice, and, besides, it attracts bees who go off somewhere and make sage honey—but it is one herb I rarely use.

Tarragon imparts a delicate flavor and is excellent with poultry. If I roast a turkey or chicken without dressing, I stuff two or three sprigs of tarragon in the cavity of the bird.

Thyme and fish go together. Thyme is added to a bouquet garni for stews and soups and marinades.

Basil is indispensable to the Italian cuisine. I use it in almost all tomato dishes and find it a perfect complement to lamb.

Savory, both winter and summer, is good with beans. A pinch of savory added to green beans will perk them up. Bean soup and baked beans rise above the pedestrian level with a little savory added to the pot.

French and Italian cooks love rosemary. The French add rosemary to green peas, and season lamb and rabbit stews with it. Italians use rosemary in many poultry dishes as well as with lamb.

In our kitchen, dill provides more than a flavoring for pickles and dilly beans. Fresh dill leaves, chopped and sprinkled on potato salad, will add a fillip. Dill and fish are good companions—dill and salmon are practically lovers. We usually get two crops of dill, planting the first in spring and the second in midsummer.

Marjoram is similar to oregano, but is not as robust an herb as oregano. It is good with beef and makes a nice addition to meat loaf and meatballs.

Oregano is certainly well known as *the* Italian seasoning. Its vigorous flavor lies at the heart of southern Italian dishes. Greeks use it in moussaka and other eggplant recipes.

Bouquet garni is simply a combination of herbs, usually parsley, tarragon, basil, savory, and thyme. Sometimes a bay leaf is added. Fines herbes should be a mixture of such herbs as parsley, chervil, tarragon, and chives. An omelet is improved with a touch of fines herbes, either fresh or dried, and they will help sauces and gravies with poultry and fish. I like a tiny pinch in most vegetables—but have a care! Too much gets to be too much very quickly.

American cooks rarely use fennel, but my grandmother never cooked pork without the addition of fennel. She always added it to her own homemade sausage. It will cut the greasiness of pork and impart a hint of anise flavoring.

Mint likes a cool, moist environment and should be rigorously contained to keep it from taking over a garden. We grow it—actually, it grows abundantly by itself—in a shady area by a stone walk below the kitchen deck. You will find many varieties of mint if you look around—peppermint, lemon mint, apple mint, spearmint, Corsican mint, and even bergamot. We grow spearmint for mint juleps on Derby Day and apple mint for fruit compotes and iced tea.

Because herbs flavor and perk up foods, the addition of salt should be kept to a minimum. Herbs often will do the job of salt, and will benefit digestion as well, but once more: Use herbs judiciously. Never let them overwhelm the flavor of foods.

A word on spices: Use only freshly ground pepper, and use it far more than salt. We are fond of Louisiana dishes, so crushed red pepper and chili powder are staples on my shelf of spices. You can't make a good gumbo without them.

Watch out for cinnamon. It is a strong spice, to be used with great discretion.

Nutmeg is more versatile than cinnamon. The French use it with meat cookery, and I like to add nutmeg to fresh peaches or in a peach pie.

Cloves have all kinds of uses. I like to decorate a ham with cloves before baking. Onions stuck with cloves have a nice affinity with baked pork. Cloves go into mixed pickling spices. Children stick cloves into oranges and lemons, let them dry, and give them to grandmothers and favorite aunts to hang in closets.

The list of herbs and spices is long. Whole books and compendiums have been written about them since the days of the Egyptians and Greeks, and I have touched on only a few here. Have I warned often enough about too free a hand? Used with careful judgment, they will add character to many bland dishes.

Now for a few recipes I didn't want to leave out.

Spicy Tomato Catsup

Wash and coarsely chop eight pounds of ripe tomatoes. Cook them until soft, and run them through a food mill, straining out all the seeds and skins. This should make two quarts of tomato purée. Put the purée in an enamel kettle with one cup cider vinegar, three tablespoons salt, two tablespoons allspice, one tablespoon dry mustard, one teaspoon black pepper, and one-half teaspoon ground red pepper. Bring the mixture to a boil, and simmer for two to three hours, stirring frequently. Seal mixture in hot sterilized pint jars. This catsup makes an excellent cocktail sauce for shrimp or raw oysters.

Chili Sauce

Scald, core, peel, and chop enough ripe tomatoes to make four quarts, and dump them in an enamel roasting pan. Add two cups chopped onions, two cups chopped sweet red peppers, three chopped small hot peppers, one cup sugar, three tablespoons salt, one tablespoon mustard seeds, one tablespoon celery seed, and two and one-half cups cider vinegar. Mix the ingredients thoroughly, and simmer in a 275° oven until as thick as desired. This takes about two hours. Stir frequently to prevent sticking. Pour into hot sterilized pint jars; adjust tops and process ten minutes in boiling water bath. This recipe yields about eight pints.

Peach Chutney

Put five pounds of ripe peaches that have been peeled, stoned, and chopped into an enamel roasting pan. Add one cup of chopped onions, one clove of crushed garlic, and one four-ounce package crystallized ginger, also chopped. Mix in one tablespoon chili powder, two tablespoons mustard seeds, one tablespoon salt, one quart apple cider vinegar, and one pound brown sugar. Put the chutney in a 275° oven, and simmer it until thick, stirring at half-hour intervals. It will take one and one-half to two hours. Pour the chutney into hot sterilized pint jars, leaving one-quarter inch head space. Adjust tops, and process ten minutes in boiling water bath. There should be five pints of chutney.

Some years ago my daughter-in-law Gina worked as a hostess for Colonial Williamsburg. Instead of brown-bagging for lunch, she and her sister hostesses brought munchies that could be nibbled at between tour groups. Gina acquired this recipe from one of her friends. She never has written it down, but she has shared it with the family, and it has become a party favorite.

Gina's Dip

Soften eight ounces of cream cheese, and mix in two tablespoons dry white wine and four teaspoons mild curry powder. Mix and beat with a fork until the cheese is smooth and creamy. Mound the cream cheese in a dome on a pretty plate, and spoon one-half pint of chutney on top. (See chutney recipe, above.) Chop finely one bunch of small green onions and their green tops, and sprinkle over the top of the chutney. Chill thoroughly, and serve with melba toast. Supply a butter spreader.

Potato Salad

Boil four medium potatoes in their jackets until just soft. Plunge them in cold water, and cool them enough to handle. Do not chill them. Skin the potatoes, and cut them in one-inch cubes. While they are still quite warm, dribble enough vinaigrette dressing (recipe for Sauce Vinaigrette, page 48) to lightly cover all the pieces of potato. Add one stalk of celery, chopped; one medium onion, chopped; one tablespoon prepared mustard; salt and pepper. You may also add sliced green olives or chopped dill pickle. If the pickle is omitted, add a tablespoon of snipped fresh dill leaves. Mix in enough mayonnaise to coat the potatoes, and chill the salad.

Hash Brown Turnips

Peel and quarter four or five medium turnips, place in an enamel pot (metal containers will discolor the turnips), and cover with water. Add salt, and boil the turnips until soft. Brown one strip of bacon, and drain it on a paper towel. In the remaining bacon drippings sauté one medium onion, sliced, until transparent. Drain the turnips in a colander, and add them to the onions in the pan. Sprinkle with freshly ground black pepper and stir; mash the turnips and onions until they are slightly browned. Crumble the bacon on top, and serve at once.

Our trilingual Mila, the daughter of a Spanish diplomatic family based in Madrid, is the wife of our youngest son, Kevin. She learned from her grandmother and her mother how to cook many of the traditional Spanish dishes. As long as I supply her with saffron, she will prepare paella for us. It is a veritable feast. She has explained that there are more variations of the dish than there are provinces of Spain, but Mila's own recipe is typical of paella as it is made in Madrid.

Mila's Paella

Bone, skin, and cut up a two-pound chicken. Heat two to three tablespoons of olive oil in a skillet, and slightly brown the chicken. Meanwhile, in a Dutch oven melt butter the size of a walnut, and add one big onion, chopped; two sweet red peppers and two sweet green peppers, seeded and cut in strips; one-half pound chorizo, sliced. Stir and cook until the vegetables are soft. Add the chicken and six big ripe tomatoes, skinned and chopped; three cloves of garlic, minced; salt and pepper; and three tablespoons fresh parsley, minced. Stir one teaspoon saffron in one-half cup of homemade chicken broth until the saffron is dissolved. Add two cups of rice to the chicken and vegetables, and let it mix with the other ingredients. Add one cup of fresh green peas and one to one and one-half cups of chicken broth, along with the saffron mixture. Mix well, cover the pot, and let the paella simmer for twenty minutes or until the rice is done. Add two pounds of large cooked shrimp, heat through, and then let the paella rest for several minutes. Serve it in a paella dish. Decorate the top with strips of pimiento, olives, and a few shrimp.

Marie's Cannelloni

Béchamel Sauce: Melt three tablespoons butter or margarine, and add three tablespoons flour, stirring and blending thoroughly. Slowly add one cup hot chicken broth and one cup light cream. Stir and cook until the sauce thickens. Add salt to taste, and stir in one-half cup grated Parmesan cheese. Set aside.

Filling: Mix three cups coarsely ground cooked turkey or chicken (as much dark meat as possible) with two tablespoons grated onion and two tablespoons parsley. Add one-third cup of the Béchamel Sauce, and mix together thoroughly.

Tomato Sauce: Mix sixteen ounces tomato sauce with one crushed garlic clove and two pinches basil.

Pasta: Cook eight large pasta tubes (usually sold as manicotti) in four quarts boiling water eight to ten minutes. The pasta should be rubbery but still underdone. Plunge the tubes in cold water. When they are cooled, drain thoroughly and stuff with the filling. An iced tea spoon works well for this job. Cover the bottom of a rectangular baking dish with half of the Tomato Sauce, lay the stuffed pasta on top of the sauce, and cover with remaining Tomato Sauce. Spoon on the remaining Béchamel Sauce, and sprinkle liberally with grated Parmesan cheese. Cover with aluminum foil, and bake in a moderate oven forty to forty-five minutes. Wait ten minutes before serving.

Chicken Liver Pâté

Place one pound of chicken livers in a colander, and rinse them thoroughly. Pat them dry, and cut them in half. Sauté the livers and a couple of tablespoons of grated onion in four tablespoons of butter or margarine. Add three anchovy fillets, and stir until they dissolve. Sauté gently until the chicken livers are no longer pink inside but are still soft. Pour all ingredients, including all the butter in the pan, into a blender container; add two tablespoons brandy, one-quarter teaspoon dry mustard, and about one-half teaspoon salt. Purée the mixture, and taste for seasoning. A pinch of tarragon does no harm. Put the mixture in a crock, and refrigerate for several hours.

Chicken Livers with Mushrooms

Rinse under cold water one pound of chicken livers, and pat them dry. Sauté the livers and one-quarter pound of mushrooms in four tablespoons of butter. Add two tablespoons of finely chopped onions or scallions. Cook for about five minutes, stirring frequently. Sprinkle with one tablespoon of flour, and stir until the flour browns a bit. Gradually add one cup of chicken bouillon, stirring until smooth. Add a pinch of tarragon and salt and pepper to taste. Simmer gently for ten or fifteen minutes. Serve over rice.

Rock Cornish Hens

We find that one rock cornish hen will feed two people generously. If you are feeding football players or young sons, you will need one hen for each person served. Wash and pat dry the hens inside and outside. Sprinkle the cavities lightly with salt, and add a pinch of tarragon or one sprig of fresh tarragon. You may add the liver also; it imparts a nice flavor. Truss the birds, and rub the breasts with salt and a little tarragon and softened butter or margarine. Place the birds in a shallow casserole with one pat of butter under each bird. Pour into the casserole enough dry white wine to come up to one-fourth of an inch in depth. Bake in a moderate oven, basting every fifteen to twenty minutes with the juices in the casserole. It will take forty-five minutes to an hour for them to be nicely brown and succulent. With poultry shears, cut the hens in half, and arrange them cut-side down on a bed of rice. Serve the sauce separately.

Ham Mousse

Measure three cups ground cooked ham. Add two teaspoons prepared mustard, two or three tablespoons grated onion, two tablespoons minced parsley, and two tablespoons dry sherry. Mix thoroughly. Soften two envelopes of gelatin in one-fourth cup cold water, and dissolve the gelatin in one cup of boiling chicken broth. Stir the gelatin and broth into the ham, mix well, and chill. Fold in one cup of sour cream.

Oil a one-and-one-half quart mold, fill it with the Ham Mousse, and chill it for several hours until it is firm. Unmold the mousse on a chilled round platter, and garnish with small tomatoes stuffed with chicken salad or with deviled eggs and parsley sprigs.

Pork Chops in Barbecue Sauce

Trim away as much fat as possible from four (one-inch-thick) loin pork chops. Spray a skillet with vegetable cooking spray, and brown the chops on both sides. Into an eight-ounce can of tomato sauce, mix one tablespoon Worcestershire sauce, one-quarter teaspoon hot pepper sauce, a little salt, and a pinch of oregano. Pour this sauce over the chops, cover the skillet, and simmer for thirty or forty minutes or until the chops are tender. Serve with the sauce poured over them. Baked beans and fried apples or hot applesauce with a sprinkling of nutmeg are complements.

Roast Pork Shoulder or Ham

Remove the skin and as much fat as possible from a five-pound fresh ham or pork shoulder. Let it stand at room temperature for one hour. Rub the meat with salt and one or two tablespoons crushed fennel seed. Add to the roasting pan two or three small whole onions stuck with three whole cloves. Put the roast in a 325° oven, and roast about thirty minutes. Pour one cup of dry white wine over the roast, and continue baking, basting every thirty or forty minutes with the juices in the pan until the pork is done. Use a meat thermometer to be sure. Remove the roast to a platter, and let it rest for thirty minutes before carving.

Degrease the juices in the pan; remove the onions, and place them around the roast. Pour one cup of water into the pan, and boil the mixture over high heat, stirring up all the brown bits in the pan. Taste the sauce for seasoning, and add salt, if necessary. Serve the sauce separately.

Veal Loin Chops

Trim the tough skin from four veal chops, and dust the chops with flour, basil, salt, and pepper. Heat one generous tablespoon olive oil in a skillet, and brown the chops on both sides. Do not overcook. Remove the chops, pour one-third cup of dry white wine into the skillet, and boil up the liquid while stirring up the brown bits in the bottom of the pan. Replace the chops, turn the heat down low, and simmer the chops two or three minutes in the sauce. Serve the chops with the sauce ladled over them.

Pot Roast

Heat two tablespoons olive oil or cooking oil in a Dutch oven, and brown a three- or four-pound rump or boneless chuck roast on all sides. Remove the pot from the fire, and add one cup of claret or Burgundy and one cup of water. Add to the pot two onions in quarters, four carrots cut into fat strips, two stalks of celery with tops cut into one-inch-long pieces, a bay leaf, a pinch or two of thyme, two sprigs of parsley, and a pig's foot split in half. Add salt to taste. Cover the Dutch oven tightly and bake the roast slowly in a 275° oven for two hours. Add three tablespoons of brandy and continue baking for another hour or until the roast is very tender. Remove pig's foot and bay leaf. Place roast on a platter surrounded by the vegetables; degrease sauce, and serve separately.

Foie de Veau Pietri (Calf's Liver)

Rinse and pat dry four slices of calf's liver. Sprinkle lightly with flour and salt and pepper. Melt two pats of butter or margarine in a skillet, and sauté one sliced onion and one-half cup sliced mushrooms until they give up their juice. Push the vegetables to the sides of the skillet, and gently brown the liver. The liver should be pink inside when pricked with a fork. Add one-half cup dry white wine, one tablespoon chopped fresh parsley, and a pinch of thyme. Simmer the liver for five minutes, stirring the sauce frequently. The liver should be soft and still a bit pink inside. Place on a warm platter, pour the onion and mushroom sauce over all, and garnish with parsley.

Calf's Liver

One pound of sliced liver will feed four to six persons. Rinse the slices in cold water, pat dry, and carefully remove skin and tubes. Roll each slice in seasoned flour. Heat two tablespoons butter or margarine in a pan and quickly brown the liver—no more than three minutes for each side. Remove liver and set aside. In the same pan on low heat, cook one-fourth cup of finely chopped scallions or onions until soft. Add one-half cup of dry red wine (claret or light Burgundy); stir in all the brown bits from the pan. Replace liver and simmer five minutes. It should be soft and slightly pink inside. Place on a warm platter, pour the wine sauce over it, and garnish with parsley.

Daughter-in-law Sharon, who brings the gift of imagination to her kitchen, was faced one hot summer day with a bare refrigerator and no desire to cook a hot meal. This delightful recipe for chilled corned beef evolved.

Sharon's Corned Beef Loaf

Add two envelopes unflavored gelatin to one cup V-8 juice, and heat gently until the gelatin is dissolved. Blend together one cup mayonnaise and one cup of V-8 juice, and combine with gelatin mixture. Refrigerate until syrupy. Chop one large stalk celery; add one-half cup diced dill pickles and a twelve-ounce can of corned beef. Blend all thoroughly. Add the corned beef mixture to the gelatin mixture and again blend thoroughly. Pour the completed mixture into a loaf pan, and chill several hours or until firmly set. Unmold just before serving on a bed of Bibb lettuce or parsley.

Venison Chili

Chop finely three pounds of venison cut from the neck or shoulder. This is easier to do if the meat is partly frozen. Sauté the meat in two tablespoons of oil in a heavy Dutch oven. Add one medium onion, chopped, and cook and stir until the onion is soft. Add to the meat mixture a one-pound can of chopped tomatoes, a few drops of hot pepper sauce, and salt to taste. Add two tablespoons chili powder and one tablespoon of cumin. Cover the pot and simmer until the meat is tender—about forty-five minutes to an hour. Stir periodically. Add two large cans of red kidney beans, and simmer until the beans are heated through. Freeze any leftovers. The chili is better the second time around.

INDEX

A Pinch of This
And a Soupçon of That

Text composed in Sabon by
Akra Data
Printed by
Arcata Graphics—Kingsport
on
Bellebrook Laid Ivory
Bound by
Arcata Graphics—Kingsport
in Taratan Bond Leather
and Elephant Hide